www.SayYesInstitute.com

The**DreamBoss**

Powerful ◆ Positive ◆ Professional

By Carrie Stack, M.Ed.

DEDICATION

PBJ

You modeled and taught what it means to be a powerful, positive, and professional leader, helping so many of us become better at what we do, and how we do it.

Thank you for the impact you have had, and continue to have, on so many lives. It would be a better world if everyone had the privilege of starting a career with the experience of a "PBJ" kind of boss.

CONTENTS

ACKNOWLEDGMENTS

"Do not be concerned about others not appreciating you.
Be concerned about your not appreciating others."
~Confucius

The acknowledgements section could be overwhelming because in my coaching, training and consulting, I have had the privilege of working with thousands of people around professional and personal growth. They have all contributed to the evolution of my work and this book is an extension of countless hours of individual and group work focused on building emotional intelligence skills.

I have come to understand that people, regardless of age, education, experience, position etc., are simply looking to live peaceful, happy, and fulfilling lives. People want to feel connected and valued, with the ability to positively contribute to the world around them. It is an amazing opportunity to share tools/strategies that could contribute to someone's life experience and I am grateful for the consistent willingness people have to try on new ways of thinking about their lives, experiences, perspectives, and relationships.

To past/ current clients: Thank you for giving me the opportunity to cross paths with you on this journey, it has been an honor. To the individuals that have sat in my office for coaching, the groups of managers/supervisors I have provided with coaching/training, and all of the larger teams that I have trained, please know your energy, openness, and honesty as you explored new tool and strategies are the reasons this book was written.

I have appreciated your ongoing feedback, both immediate as well as years later, about what worked, what helped you, and what you struggled with. Your input helped develop and expand these tools in order to ensure they are as useful as possible, to as many as possible.

Thank you for your willingness to allow humor in to this equation. Thank you for the laughter, the openness to see imperfections, and for being open to trying new ways of being, in order to experience new ways of living. I couldn't do this work if there wasn't room to laugh, so thank you for giving me lots of space to find and share the humor!

And, to those that I have yet to have the pleasure of meeting: It is my hope you found something useful in this book and you will be trying out some new skills/tools in your world. I look forward to the possibility of our paths crossing in the future because I'm going to need you for the next book!

Finally, thank you to Shelagh Braley and Bill Starr for working tirelessly to create and build a powerful platform for people to reach their goals and live life fully. Please know I am grateful for your endless support, encouragement, excitement, and editing as we got *The Dream Boss* ready to meet the world. (And I am very excited to have reached another one of my goals on mylifelist.org!)

1 FROM THE AUTHOR

"People travel to wonder at the height of the mountains,
at the huge waves of the seas,
at the long course of the rivers,
at the vast compass of the ocean,
at the circular motion of the stars,
and yet, they pass by themselves without wondering."
~St. Augustine

"And yet, they pass by themselves without wondering." If you are a leader, contrary to the quote, many of you have probably done a lot of wondering. You have spent countless hours lost in a state of perpetual wonder around your role and what you are trying to do. You have wondered about how to do the best job possible, wondered about the seemingly endless challenges you have faced, and especially wondered how to crack the mystery around why sometimes it feels like it's all coming together, while other days it appears to fall miserably short. You have wondered about how to be better, how to be more effective, how to be more inspiring, and how to generally just be more. You have wondered how you got here, wondered if you even like it here, and wondered if this is worth it at all. One thing you don't need to wonder about is whether there are a lot of pieces to this leadership puzzle, because there are. The good news is they can and will fit together, if you only take the time to understand how.

The Dream Boss comes from training and coaching countless managers/supervisors, and their teams, around how to effectively build emotional intelligence skills (or people skills). The skills and tools in *The Dream Boss* have an audience beyond those with a boss title on a business card because at some point, in some way, everyone is "in charge" somewhere in their lives.

People are supervising, leading, or managing people at work, at school, at church, in the community, and within a family. Bottom line, whoever you are, wherever, you are, you have a lot of people in your world and it takes infinite skills to manage all of those relationships in a positive way. People bring joy, laughter, and infinite "wow" moments into our lives. But those same people also have the capacity to bring challenges, stress, and frustration. Emotional intelligence skills are never centered on changing/shifting/fixing the other person, because that doesn't work. These skills and tools are focused on helping you to handle whatever situation you are in, so however challenged you may be, you are able to successfully maintain a powerful, positive, and professional state.

This book provides easy-to-use, accessible, and transferable strategies to apply and use in whatever circles they are leading. As a trainer and a coach, I am grateful for the extensive, ongoing feedback I have received over the years around these tools, including how to best capture and present them. I hope you are able to find something in this book that contributes to the growth of *The Dream Boss* living inside of you.

Much success,
Carrie

2 INTRODUCTION

*"The real voyage of discovery consists
NOT in seeking new lands
but seeing with new eyes."*
~Marcel Proust

People want to be successful when they are the boss. They want to lead, manage, and supervise in a way that supports the team to reach individual and collective goals.

Unfortunately, here is where things can get tricky. People may know they want it, but they don't know how to go about doing it. People struggle to become the kind of boss they would like to be, despite putting in a lot of time, energy, and effort.

Many people have said they feel optimistic about managing the team when they are sitting at home drinking coffee, diligently developing a plan for the upcoming day. But when they get to the office, many times it flows more like a bad sitcom than the Emmy award-winning script they created hours earlier.

The morning fantasy about meeting with the team to plan the next project, with everyone excited and engaged, never quite materializes. Individual supervisions, with employees coming in prepared with thoughtful reflections of their performance and eager to look at how to improve productivity and expand their contribution to the team? Sounded hopeful, but that doesn't happen either. Appreciations, acknowledgments, and affirmations shared with reckless abandon throughout unit meetings? Nine hours at the office and there wasn't even a flicker of something positive shared by anyone, at any meeting, at any point, during the long and draining day. Nothing reflects a speck of the morning's delusional wishes, and it's only Monday.

Sound familiar? If you're a manager, leader, supervisor, or a boss in any capacity in your world, there's a good chance something about this resonates with you. For many of you, it more than resonates and it is clicking in a big, big way.

It's good to know that you're not alone, but beyond the shallow sense of peace that comes from confirmation you're in good company, this isn't good enough. You know this could be better and you could be better. You are ready to go all in with this belief because you cannot continue living this predictable, bland, and uninspired script for the rest of your days. That just cannot be an option.

You want your team to go to the next level, because you are ready to go to the next level. You are ready to admit that you want to be The Dream Boss and you are prepared to make this happen by trying some new tools, strategies and perspectives. Some of you may feel like you don't care about being a dream anything—you just want to be a halfway decent boss people don't hate, and that is fine, too. Wherever you're at, or whatever you aspire to be, if you're looking to grow, there are tools in here for you to try.

What goes into the making of a Dream Boss? There are many components to it, but it can be distilled to three areas: Powerful, Positive, and Professional.

What makes a *Dream Boss*?

>> **Powerful:** They *know* how to succeed, as well as how to support others to succeed.

>> **Positive:** They genuinely *like* who they are, what they are doing, and the people/world around them.

>> **Professional:** They consistently *model*, by what they say and what they do, boundaries, respect, and integrity.

The three components to *The Dream Boss* foundation include:

1. Powerful: KNOW

Powerful: Having great power, prestige, or influence—a leader

The Dream Boss is Powerful. This power establishes your credibility. *The Dream Boss* is comfortable owning the power that comes with being in charge. This is not about a power trip, or dangling power over the team, which some mistakenly attribute to establishing power. True power does not need to be stated.

Power is something you feel, and it comes from confidence, clarity, and vision. You trust you have what it takes to be a leader and people around you believe you can lead them. If they didn't feel you were solid in your power, they would wonder, "How can I follow you, if I don't know/trust that you know how to lead me?" It is imperative that you believe you have the ability to lead, because if you don't believe it, how would you ever convince anyone else you are qualified to be in charge?

Being Powerful is the foundation of being *The Dream Boss*.

Some examples of what being *Powerful* looks like:

>> Clear on the bigger picture (mission/vision/future)

>> Have a plan on how to achieve bigger picture

>> Solid

>> Understand the impact of power and being a leader

>> Share power, knowing that sharing it never diminishes it

>> Confident

>> Leader

>> Strong sense of ownership, responsibility, and accountability

>> Ability to adeptly celebrate/acknowledge successes, as well as support team through any challenges/struggles

>> Steady in a crisis

>> Competent, knowledgeable, experienced

What does being *Powerful* mean to you?

10/25/13

* Trust
* Credibility
* Working Along side your Staff.
* Knowing Your Job
* Knowledge
* Achievement

In life, where do you feel *Powerful*?

* At home.
* my office

As a leader, where do you feel *Powerful*?

* Meetings
* being able to Provide Knowledge to my staff
* my office
* When I pull up to my Branch every morning & see Gil

How would you like to expand/develop in this area?

more
Confidence

2. Positive: LIKE

Positive: having a good effect, favorable - a role model marked by optimism

The Dream Boss is Positive. There is an energy that comes from the positive that draws people in, builds relationships, and cultivates investment. Being positive is appealing and focusing on the positive is an energy boost. People want to be around positive people and this pull has a tremendous effect on the culture and climate when that positive person is the boss.

Some of you may feel resistant or even a little cynical around a focus on the positive because of past experiences with people deemed too nice, or who you believed were taken advantage of because of their good nature. Before going any further, it's important to clarify: Being positive is not about smiling a lot while ignoring or hiding from issues. It is not about being a Pollyanna who believes all is well, all the time, with everyone. It should never be confused with weakness, passivity, naiveté, or a displaced desire to be liked by everyone on the team, at any cost. Certainly not every day is about smiles, hugs, sunshine, and high fives. There are many days, weeks, or painfully long stretches of time that feel like they hold none of those things, yet it is still possible for a leader to be fundamentally positive.

Being a positive leader is about looking for what is right, what is working, what is getting done, what is going well, and what is succeeding. It means being a leader who builds upon the strengths of individuals, teams, and systems in a way that encourages growth and movement.

Being positive means the spotlight is on supporting success, while challenges and obstacles are approached with the intention of addressing them, and then getting right back on board with moving, growing and achieving!

Being positive is a foundational framework that shapes how a person moves through the world, and impacts how someone both interprets and experiences daily life. A positive lens not only serves to enhance your life, but has the capacity to positively touch the lives of all of those around you. Quite simply, when people are grounded in the positive, they seek it out and celebrate it wherever they are, including at work.

When the leader is positive, it has a tremendous impact on the team. Being positive is a pivotal element to incorporate into your efforts to become *The Dream Boss!*

Some examples of what being *Positive* looks like:

>> Optimistic

>> Look for what is right, what is working, what is getting done

>> Believe in employees

>> Enjoy the work

>> Strength-based approach

>> Accessible and approachable (smile, laugh, outgoing)

>> Trust in self, in staff, in work, in bigger vision

>> Forward moving, future focused

>> Steady, calm, even keeled, on daily basis as well as in crisis

>> Solid perspective

>> Realistic

>> Generous with appreciation, gratitude, and thanks

>> Support learning, especially during challenges/obstacles/failures

>> Celebrate successes, acknowledge contributions

What does being *Positive* mean to you?

Smile! Smile! Smile!
Greet
take time to listen

In life, where do you feel *Positive*?

Home/work

As a leader, where do you feel *Positive*?

Coaching
helping

How would you like to expand/develop in this area?

Being able to handle change more
positive way.

3. Professional: MODEL

Professional: exhibiting a courteous, conscientious, and generally businesslike manner in the workplace

The Dream Boss is Professional. Many leaders will say, "Of course I'm professional, since you must be professional if you're in charge!" Not necessarily.

It's important to remember being professional is not determined by what you wear, where your office is, or what title/position is printed on your business card. It is not about your degree, or the length of time you have been in the job. It's not about how many people you manage, or how many meetings you run. It is not about the things people typically rattle off to prove they are professional.

Being professional is more complicated than people realize. It's actually about how you move through the days, every day, as the boss. It is about how you navigate emotions—your own as well as those of your team—that surface while on the job. Being professional is about how you treat all employees, even the ones you may not like. Being professional is about how you communicate, model behaviors, maintain boundaries, and create a climate and culture of equality that fosters growth and productivity.

A lot of people assume they must have somehow mastered the skill of being professional, just by nature of climbing the career ladder and becoming the boss. Unfortunately, you don't have to look very hard to see that's not how it works, as being professional does not innately accompany any specific role or job description. This final piece actually builds upon mastery of the first two. When you become comfortable being Powerful, and have fully embraced the Positive, you have the foundation to focus on claiming the final piece as you become Professional.

Some examples of what being *Professional* looks like:

>> Clear boundaries

>> High standards/expectations

>> Consistent

>> Equality (no "double standards" or hypocrisy)

>> Fair

>> Attention to detail

>> Ethical

>> Ownership, responsibility, accountability

>> Expertly handle emotions (self and others)

>> Model professionalism for staff

>> Strong communicator

>> Investment in growth/learning/education

>> Transparent (no hidden agendas)

What does being *Professional* mean to you?

Looking Professional
Confidence
Body Language

In life, where do you feel *Professional*?

Work
When Wearing my GI Shirt

As a leader, where do you feel *Professional*?

Work
When wearing my GI Shirt

How would you like to expand/develop in this area?

accessorize more

3 PURPOSE OF *THE DREAM BOSS*

*"When we seek to discover the best in others,
we somehow bring out the best in ourselves."*
~William Arthur Ward

As you read this book, do a little research of your own around some of these areas. Try asking someone, "Have you ever had a terrible boss? A boss who was a real nightmare to work for and you couldn't get out fast enough?" You will probably find most people reply, "Yes! I certainly have!" Then you will hear story after story about what the boss(es) did, or did not do, to secure a top notch spot on the, "Worst Boss Ever" list. You may even have that list, too. It could be going back to your first job, 15 years old and selling pizza, but you remember all the gory details of working for someone who embodied what doesn't work when you're the boss. If you are fortunate enough to not have any direct experience in this area, you have certainly endured endless tales of bad boss woes from all of your nearest and dearest.

After establishing what doesn't work in a boss, notice what happens when you ask people, "Have you ever had an amazing boss? A boss that you will forever remember and appreciate for what they did and how they did it?" As you listen notice the smiles, the faraway look in the eyes, and the nostalgic tone in the voice (or, if it's a current boss, the way the voice goes up a few octaves with excitement, glee and a little flaunting!). People typically don't have as many examples of the boss(es) that rocked their worlds, but it is clear they cherish the ones they have. Perhaps you aren't even with us right now, because you have a faraway twinkle in your eye, remembering the time you worked for someone who firmly secured a spot at the top of your "Best Of" list!

What is up with this managing/supervising thing? Why does it seem to happen so easily for some, while others endlessly struggle with it? It's a fascinating conundrum because people skills are the foundation to successfully managing and supervising, yet we don't seem to teach, or even talk about, people skills. We just hope people with a title will somehow innately know what to do and connect the dots in a profound and powerful way as they lead teams to greatness. At this point it's becoming clear all the hoping isn't translating to much and we might need to do more than just hope. It could be time to start doing things differently.

Where should we start doing things differently? We could start with preparation, training, and support. If there isn't a lot of training or preparation on how to lead, then how do people become the leader? For a lot of people it looks something like this, "Great news! If you show up, do a good job, and give everything you have, you will be promoted! You will run this department (team, program, unit). Play your cards right and you'll become the boss of the people that used to be your peers!"

The rest of that statement should be, "But, we regret to inform you we won't be able to help you develop your management, leadership, or supervision skills, and we don't really have any thoughts on how to do it, or how to do it better. Please just try really hard every day and do the best you can!" Or maybe it's more like this, "Congratulations! You are brilliant and you know your content, so you're hired and you'll be the boss now! See you Monday when you meet your big team and take over this troubled department!"

This person has the education and experience for the content part of the work, but content is only half of the equation. What about the process piece? That is where the team needs a leader's skill, and that crucial piece is often missing.

Working with hundreds of managers/supervisors and teams around how to develop emotional intelligence skills (also known as people skills or soft skills), I have been asked over and over, "What are the key things that you wish managers, leaders and supervisors knew?" I looked at my work over the years and targeted the pieces that kept emerging. Those pieces, and the models created to help people in those areas, became the foundation for *The Dream Boss*.

This book isn't just for leaders/managers, as it is filled with tips that could be relevant for all people. These are tools everyone could add to their tool box with the potential to improve their overall lives, as well as increase productivity, satisfaction, and professional success. Whoever you are, you are managing/ leading or supervising on some level, somewhere in your life. Maybe it is a department at work, or the parents at your child's school. Maybe you run a multimillion dollar department, or perhaps you supervise a team at an after-school program. You could have two part-time people you manage, or a volunteer group of 800 that you want to take to the next level. The skills in this book are relevant for people who cross paths with other people, so if you have people in your life, there is something in here for you.

This book is the result of people over the years saying that they wanted a guide book, or the play book, or a cheat sheet on how to be a better manager. Based on all the trainings, coaching and supervisions I have done with people, as well as extensive conversations I have had with both managers/supervisors as well their teams, here it is. The purpose of sharing this information is because these tools consistently appear to have interest and value for people, and perhaps most importantly, they have worked.

4 THE 'IT' FACTOR

*"If I have the belief that I can do it,
I shall surely acquire the capacity to do it
even if I may not have it at the beginning."*
~Mahatma Gandhi

The majority of our lives are spent in the workplace and we all deserve, including managers/supervisors, to have successful, effective, and positive experiences at work. I've never met a supervisor who wakes up and decides that today s/he will thoughtfully and intentionally move into the day with the goal of wreaking havoc on staff. Nobody heads in to the office thinking, "I'd really like to make the life of every member of my team a living hell today. My goal is to see how many people will think about quitting. I will be really successful if more than 80 percent of the team actually logs on to a job search site today at lunch!"

No, that is never the case and it may surprise you to discover many managers and supervisors are filled with daily stress and anxiety over how to do a better job. Even the boss winning top billing in your "Worst Ever" category was actually trying to do a good job. It may be hard for you to believe, but even those bosses wanted to be successful at positively leading the team. What is the problem then? Everyone is doing the best they can with what they have, but sometimes people simply don't have the right tools.

What are the "right tools?" What are the successful managers doing? I have had the remarkable experience of asking hundreds and hundreds of people the same two questions, and regardless of the group demographics, received similar answers. I've asked people 18 years old, working after school for three years, and people 68 years old, working, as one woman proudly proclaimed, "For two of your lifetimes!" The experiences and insights people have shared are consistent across age, ethnicity, gender, income, education, title, or position.

Before you see what people shared, first see what you think in the activity below, because this is the fastest and easiest way to ensure you will be open to the tools/strategies in the book.

Action: The "It" Factor

PART 1

Have you ever had a terrible supervisor? A supervisor who can barely inspire you to blink and breathe, never mind go to the next level professionally! A supervisor you will forever remember because he/she was the living embodiment of what does not work? A supervisor who asked you to come in on a Saturday and your first thought was, "Are you kidding? Not unless this is explicitly stated on my job description!" No actual names are needed here, but what did this boss do or not do, to make them so memorable in this way? Can you define it?

On the next page, take a minute and write down the traits that come to mind. (*You actually need to do this, because activities in the book only work if you do them!)

What does NOT work:

Based on hundreds and hundreds of replies, from people 18 years old to 82 years old, it's fascinating how similar the lists always are. Every list has some combination/variation of the traits and skills below.

Group-identified examples of what does NOT work:

>> Hypocritical/double standards
>> Entitled/inflated self-importance
>> Has favorites, and/or targets
>> Doesn't listen
>> Never says "thank you"
>> Moody/angry/snaps/yells
>> Doesn't do what they say they will, lies
>> Negative
> Takes all the credit/shifts all blame or responsibility
>> Promises things they don't or won't do/no follow through
>> Ineffective communicator
>> Unprofessional
>> Poor boundaries
>> Doesn't seek input or feedback
>> Condescending
>> Believes they are better/more important
>> No structure
>> Hostile/cold/distant/detached
>> Dismissive
>> Micromanaging
>> Tells, never asks
>> Egocentric/narcissistic
>> Unpredictable/inconsistent
>> Not mission focused/lack of vision or bigger picture
>> Explosive/tantrums
>> Overwhelmed/can't perform job requirements

PART 2

After naming what doesn't work, now we want to name what does work. We will now define the illustrious "It" Factor.

Have you ever had a supervisor that was magic and you knew you were in the midst of something amazing? It was as if you hit the lottery and you knew it. Matter of fact, the whole team felt lucky and people actually enjoyed the work and working together! When you talked about your work, you knew others envied you and you knew this manager would make the short list of "WOW" bosses that you would have in your lifetime. You thought this person was amazing at his/her job, and the way they did *their* job, made you love *your* job. If you were asked to come in on a Saturday, you'd say, "Absolutely ... and I'll stop and pick up the bagels/coffee on my way in!" They embodied the "It" factor and became the benchmark for what *The Dream Boss* means to you.

What was "it?" What did they do that made them memorable? Right now, take a minute to define the traits, skills, strengths, attributes and actions of your "WOW" boss.

For the few of you out there that have NOT had a magical boss, think about bosses that friends/family have had that fall in to this category. Even if you haven't directly experienced it, you know people that have- because they told you all about their "amazing" boss, all the time, so use their experiences to help you do this next activity. How do I know they incessantly talked about their amazing boss? Because people always do.

The 'It' Factor:

Based on the list below, the boss that stands out and is held in high regard by so many clearly embodies what it means to be Powerful, Positive, and Professional.

Group-identified examples of the 'It' Factor:

>> Respect
>> Approachable/available
>> Appreciative/Says "thank you"
>> Constructive feedback
>> Positive attitude
>> Collaborates
>> Listens
>> Cares/invested
>> Boundaries
>> Trust/hands off
>> Empathetic
>> Passion for work
>> Professionalism
>> Laughs/happy/sense of fun
>> Energetic
>> Willing to work with team
>> Follows same standards, norms, and expectations as team
>> Equal treatment of all staff
>> Inspires/motivates people
>> Organized
>> Solid/stable/consistent
>> Ability to apologize/admit mistakes/learns from challenges
>> Mentor
>> Willing to do what needs to be done/jumps in/pitches in
>> Vision
>> Commitment to professional development and growth
>> Accessible
>> Integrity/word is "good"

Why do this activity? To help people understand, from their own experiences, they already know what works, and what doesn't work. Establishing these "norms" about what makes an effective supervisor, from personal experience, enables people to look at things through a different lens. It enables people to reflect on their actions/behaviors, as well as opens the door to recognize individual strengths and areas for growth. Self-reflection is the only way to figure out what you already know, and where you may want to grow.

It's important to acknowledge we most likely will find ourselves on both lists, as we all have areas of success/mastery and we are all capable of demonstrating less than desirable management/ leadership skills. And yes, "all of us" actually includes you, too.

The question becomes, if we are on both lists, what do we do? How do we make sure that we're developing and building more of the "It" Factor skills of *The Dream Boss*, and not staying stuck in the, "what doesn't work" category? Are the bosses who have the "It" Factor perfect? No, they are actually far from it. Sometimes they messed up, some days they dropped the ball. They have even been wrong, or snappy, or limited in their vision, or their skills. They still have "It" but it's not because they are perfect.

They embody the "It" Factor because even when they were imperfect, they handled it with finesse.

If they messed up, they owned it. If they dropped the ball, they named it. If they were wrong or snappy, they apologized and didn't attempt to minimize or deflect what they did. They successfully handle and manage their emotions, and if/when they don't, they were quick to recognize it and respond appropriately to own, address, and apologize for their actions. The "It" Factor isn't about only having powerful, positive, professional, or perfect emotions; it's about handling your emotions powerfully, positively, professionally, and perfectly.

We all have an innate understanding of what the magic is, which is fabulous. It's great to name who the great ones are, but isn't it even better to be one? Do you want to be one of the supervisors/managers that has the "It" Factor? Do you want to move through the world with the "WOW" factor connected to your name?

Of course you do, so let's figure out how to do that.

5 DCI© MODEL

*"If you want to be successful,
know what you are doing,
love what you are doing,
and believe in what you are doing."*
~Will Rogers

The Say Yes Institute builds all coaching, training and workshops around the Define, Clarify and Implement (DCI) Model©. This three-part model was created as a powerful tool to support a thoughtful assessment of personal/professional goals, determine why those goals are important, and develop a specific plan of action to reach those goals. The DCI Model© works because it is concrete, direct, and clearly focused on developing a comprehensive strategy to reach/achieve each identified goal.

Participants are encouraged to explore the DCI Model© through a series of thought provoking questions and interactive/reflective activities. This has been proven to be an effective strategy, both with individuals and within groups, because it quickly fosters a sense of focus and inspires direct action.

The DCI Model© supports participants to formulate clear goals, as well as own clarity around their investment in reaching those goals. The steps help participants to develop a comprehensive, logical, achievable, and powerful plan of implementation which includes clear goals, timelines, plans of accountability, and tools to assess progress and validate successes. Each skill/strategy in this book will be explored through the DCI Model© in order to help frame it, give it context, and provide you with a blueprint to achieve your personal and professional success.

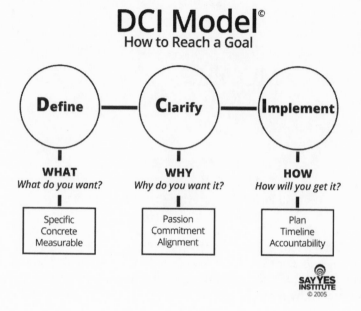

The three steps of the DCI Model© are:

Define: WHAT

This step supports exploration around the many layers to clearly define the "what" part of your goals. You need to know, specifically and concretely, exactly what you want to achieve. This covers the specific questions of "how much, how many, by when?" Your goal needs to be measurable, so you know when you reach it. Many people set goals that are generic, ambiguous, and not clearly measurable, like "be more successful." Vague goal setting translates to a vague victory. How will you know when it's time to celebrate your success if you have never clearly named what it would look like? Make sure your goal is framed in the positive, and is specific enough that you will know when you have achieved it.

Use these questions to help you define the "what" of the goal you want to reach:

What is your specfic, concrete, and measurable goal?
(How much, how many, and by when?)

What would having this mean to you, or do for you?

What is of value to you about this goal?

What does your goal look like when you've reached it, or how will you know you have reached it?

Clarify: WHY

This step illuminates the "why" part of the process and produces clarity around why you believe a goal is worth achieving and warrants your valuable time and attention. Many goals are defined on the intellectual level; however a mental belief that it is a good/positive/logical goal isn't going to be enough to get there if a person has no clear connection to the goal. If someone isn't in alignment with the goal, or the heart isn't in it, the person isn't going to do it.

The "why" will drive you forward when there are challenges/ obstacles or barriers. When a person succeeds at a goal it is often because having an authentic alignment supports focus and determination, even when there are bumps in the road. This step reminds us we invest in what we believe in and are committed to, not just what may appear logical or sound. It is the heart part of the goal that builds commitment which ultimately ensures the follow through needed to makes things happen.

Use these questions to help you clarify the "why" of the goal you want to reach:

> ### Why are you invested in reaching your goal?

> ### Why do you feel a sense of passion, commitment, or alignment around this goal?

Why is this goal a priority for you?

Why would reaching this goal be of value to you, your work, and your life?

Implement: HOW

This step encompasses the concrete "how" of your implementation plan and details specific actions needed to achieve your goal. A clear implementation plan is foundational to your success. You need to know what actions you will take, how you will take them, and how you will address possible roadblocks and challenges.

Well-formed goals, even with a high level of passion and alignment, can still idle indefinitely if there is no plan for action. It is also important to decide how, if at all, you will be accountable for reaching your goal. Some people do best with external accountability and need to build in some way to have follow-up with others, while others excel with only internal accountability. It's important to clearly name all of the components that encompass the "how" of your implementation phase.

Use these questions to help you determine a solid action/implementation plan around how you will reach your goal:

How will you develop a plan and timeline for reaching this goal?

How will you know you have achieved your goal?

How will you address any barriers, challenges, or obstacles?

How/ to whom will you be accountable?

To support maximum growth and application of new skills and tools, all activities in the book will be presented and processed through the DCI Model©. It's not enough for people to read an activity and think, "Wow, that's interesting." Thinking something is interesting isn't enough of a catalyst to trigger action and application. Simply noting something doesn't transfer to actually doing something. The goal is to have people read about an activity, try on a new perspective, and then have an immediate, executable plan to implement the activity in a concrete way.

To take it one step further, and in the interest of full transparency, the hope is you will read it, "get" it, and then head in to your world to use it! Clarity doesn't come from sitting on the couch, so the only way for you to acquire new skills and tools is for you to actually do something new. The DCI Model© will help make sure you're ready for action as you integrate these new skills and tools in to your life.

6 POWERFUL

*"Our chief want
is someone who will inspire us
to be what we know we could be."*
~Ralph Waldo Emerson

You're a leader and you're in charge. Because of your role, you have power. And because of that power, you are powerful.

It's interesting how many people in positions of power have never thought about what the word means. They have never connected the dots around what it means to have power, or how to best use that power to positively impact their world, or the people in it.

Why does that happen? How are people in positions of power so often oblivious to the kind of impact their role has on others? Through information gathered from training and coaching it seems to come down to two reasons. The first reason is typically because the person was promoted without ever receiving training on what kinds of skills are needed to successfully lead a group/team. The second reason is often because a person is incredibly knowledgeable and talented around content, or the "what" part of the job, but never received training on the process, or the "how."

Did you read that and think, *"Wait, aren't both of those reasons about lack of training?"* You are correct. There is actually one reason why people have a tough time with managing/leading others, and it comes down to lack of training. People can't give what they don't have, and they can't do what they don't know. Without being given the training, support, and skills/tools necessary to lead effectively, people will struggle. There is no mystery to what is going awry here. Leaders know it, and their teams know it, so in the best interest of all parties to fix this.

What are the kinds of things that people in leadership roles are saying? Where are leaders finding/facing struggles with their staff or teams?

Here are a few thoughts from some managers/ supervisors.

Action: What Went Wrong?

If you heard someone saying the things below, what would you be thinking? If you had to determine what may have gone awry with their leadership, what would you come up with?

What's wrong with this picture?

"I guess it (the reorganization) could be taken the wrong way, since the team didn't know the whole story. It made sense to me, but I can see how it wouldn't make sense to them, which is why we're dealing with this big crisis of trust now."
~ Director

"I feel like everything I do is wrong. It's like I can't get them (team) to take initiative and everything feels like a struggle."
~ Executive Director

"I just lay it on the line. I keep telling them what's not working, because I'm hoping they will do something differently, but nothing is changing. It's actually getting worse."
~ Team Supervisor

"We are probably in this position because I didn't handle things in the way I should have when they initially happened. I thought things would work themselves out, but they never did and I let it go for too long."
~ Manager

"I keep hoping that some people will give their notice, because I need people in here that are willing to work, and that I can work with. I know some people are dealing with a lot in their lives, but I can't keep doing their jobs. It's just too much."
~ Team Leader

Can you relate to any of these, or does any of this feel familiar to you?

In the space below, you are the coach/consultant. Write down what you think might be happening with the managers/directors/leaders.
What do you think they may be doing, or not doing, to contribute to the issues they are dealing with at work? What could be present, or absent, in the culture/climate? Where do you think leadership needs to shine the light in order to effectively address these issues?

Thoughts:

Process:

What did you come up with? In your opinion, what areas seemed to be an issue? You probably identified some of these areas:

What went wrong?

>> Lack of communication
>> Issues with ownership
>> Being negative/punitive
>> Not dealing with issues, denial, avoidance
>> Lack of vision
>> No relationships/connection to staff
>> Double standards/possible inconsistencies
>> Lack of clarity around how to support/lead/direct the team
>> Owning too much/taking on too much/doing too much

It can be easy to see what's missing when you're looking at someone else's performance, or reflecting on the struggles/challenges with someone else's team, but it is harder to see when it's your team. How do things go so wrong for so many managers and supervisors? And, more importantly, how can people work to make things better?

In all of the conversations with people around the key qualities of The Dream Boss, the most powerful leaders had one piece that emerged over and over. They had a clear, strong, consistent commitment to equality. A foundation of equality lends itself to trust, and a leader holding the trust of a group has a great deal of power.

What does equality mean? Equality means things are unequivocally equal, with all people, all the time. That is an incredibly challenging state to maintain, especially because the reality is: You don't like everyone the same. You don't find everyone equally appealing, you don't view everyone on your team in an equally favorable light, and you certainly don't think everyone on your team performs equally. You may know it, and I certainly know it, but your team will never know it.

Members of your team will never be privy to the possibility you find some people a dash more spectacular than others. To take it one step further, if it were ever revealed you had favorites, people would be beyond shocked.

The group would be floored to hear that you really don't like Myrtle or Howard and you would be fine if they searched for a new job, on company time. Nobody would ever know your true feelings, not from meetings or supervisions, nor from any of your conversations or actions, because you are a professional at handling your emotions. You are tapped in to the importance of treating everyone equally, in all ways, at all times. That ability is the sign of a mature boss and takes tremendous skill, awareness, and practice.

It takes skill to remember you are always on. When you're tired, when your car breaks down, when you're dealing with a family drama, you are still on. When you have a headache, when you're annoyed with your brother, when you find out your accountant made a significant error in your taxes, you are still on. You are the boss and people are watching everything you say, and everything you do, all the time. This has endless ramifications for you and all of your actions or reactions. Fair or unfair, you are always in a position to be held up as an example or model on how to handle yourself appropriately and act in a consistent and predictable way. The example you set is inextricably linked to how powerful you are in the eyes of your team, and your ability to adhere to principals of equality, even when tired, or stressed, or annoyed, should be considered impressive!

Beyond a commitment to equality, how can you build up your skills to own the role of being Powerful? How can you make sure you are saying and doing things that contribute to your efforts to become *The Dream Boss*? Here are four tools/strategies to help you become a more Powerful leader:

1. Leadership CHOICE: Power of Your Daily Decisions

"The better my mood is, the better the team seems to be. I used to think that my mood was a result of the day, but now I see that my mood actually sets the stage for the day. When I'm positive, everything is better and I really want to have more of those days!" ~ Assistant Director

What if the catalyst for the quality and content of your day wasn't about the luck of the draw, or the stars aligning? What if it wasn't about having perfect weather, or the right outfit, or your favorite sandwich for lunch?

What if there was no big mystery as to why some days are simply amazing, while others feel like an endless barrage of unbearable misery? What if the determining factor wasn't a hidden mystery and it was simply about you?

The great news is you are the one with the power to determine what your day will hold. You may not be aware of this, but every single day you make choices which determine your day. You choose how you are going to experience every conversation, exchange, and event in your world. This isn't a secret inside scoop that only some people are told, while the rest are left in the dark. The fact is, every day you are in control of what you choose to focus on, and how you choose to direct your energy.

Another way to think about this is: Every day you take countless positions on people, events, experiences, etc., and then you set out to prove your position is correct by the evidence you gather during the day. If you think it's going to be a great day, the team is going to do great things, and you are going to love your job, then you would be able to prove that at the end of the day because you would have collected countless examples supporting that position. If you think it's going to be a horrible day, the team is dysfunctional and lazy, you hate your job, you're underappreciated, and the world is simply a miserable place, at the end of the day you could prove that, too. You are amazing at proving your position, whatever position you take. Unfortunately, most people aren't aware of what position you are proving, and many are shocked to find they have been busy taking chronically negative or deficit-based positions on everyone and everything in their lives.

People get a little cranky when they hear this. People are very invested in believing life happens to them, not from them. People talk about their moods/attitudes as if they have no control over them, or that those moods/attitudes are inflicted upon them by outside sources. It is important to remember that nothing, no experience or action or event, has any inherent meaning, good or bad. This means we are the ones assigning meaning, and the moments of our lives are nothing more or less than the meaning we give them.

Do you see where this is going? Your focus and your energy is an ongoing choice, and the choice is solely yours. Every day your world and the people in it, including the people at work, are viewed based on how you choose to direct your energy and your focus. You take positions on people, then you give their words/actions meaning based on how you have chosen to direct your focus and energy.

To be clear, your daily choices really matter. Not understanding the importance or the implications of those choices has caused grief for many, many bosses. When you choose to focus your energy on the negative, it can create a mess—and a short memory on your end does not equal a short memory on their end. You had a bad fire back in 1988? There's still talk of that. Your little situation (or we could call it a tantrum or quasi-explosion) at a meeting three years ago? There's still residue from that around the office. That employee you gave a warning for doing something you had done the week before? You may have forgotten about it, but they still can't get over that one. You can say this isn't fair, it's ridiculous to even talk about those things because it's over, and that was an anomaly because it's not how you usually are, but guess what? As the boss, and because of your power, that's just not how it works. Your choices matter.

Whenever going into places to deal with issues of conflict, trust, low morale, or issues with the team, it typically stems from something that happened in the past that wasn't dealt with right, or fully, openly, honestly, or to completion. Why? You are powerful. What you say and do sends a message, all the time. When you're stressed, when you're cranky, when you're tired, when you're just "off," you are still sending a message. As the leader, you are still holding the identity of being powerful, whether you're in the midst of an incredibly amazing day, or a remarkably bad and uninspired day. If things are not handled well by the leader, it is a promise that it will resurface indefinitely, causing ongoing issues in the culture and climate of an organization. The decisions you make matter.

The Leadership CHOICE model can help provide a visual to how the element of choice plays out in your world every day.

Leadership CHOICE illustrates how the focus/energy of a leader can impact a team, leading to very different results. This has been used to help leaders visualize how much work a team would have to do to counterbalance a leader's negative focus. The team could still work hard to stay positive and focus on productivity and success, but it's clear they have to work so much harder just to get to where a team would be if there were a positive leader in charge. The focus and energy of a leader has a tremendous impact on a team, with very tangible results.

Action: Leadership CHOICE

Explore the Leadership CHOICE you are making on a daily basis. Where do you think you are directing your focus and energy? Is it positive or negative? How does this impact staff? What is the result?

Where do you think you are directing your focus and energy? Is it positive or negative?

How does this impact staff? What is the result?

Define: WHAT

What Leadership CHOICE will you commit to making on a daily basis?
What situations, circumstances, settings, or people will you focus on?
What will you direct your energy toward?

What is your specfic, concrete, and measurable goal?
(How much, how many, and by when?)

What would having this mean to you, or do for you?

What is of value to you about this goal?

What does your goal look like when you've reached it, or
how will you know you have reached it?

Clarify: **Why**

Why is it important to you to make this Leadership CHOICE? Why is this something you are willing to do?

Why are you invested in reaching your goal?

Why do you feel a sense of passion, commitment, or alignment around this goal?

Why is this goal a priority for you?

Why would reaching this goal be of value to you, your work, or your life?

Implement: How

How will you succeed with your new Leadership CHOICE? How will you develop a plan to make this happen?

How will you develop a plan and timeline for reaching this goal?

How will you know you have achieved your goal?

How will you address any barriers, challenges, or obstacles?

How/ to whom will you be accountable?

2. Castle of Consistency: Power of a Strong and Stable Environment

"If I had to be honest, I know that the rules probably aren't the same for everyone on my team and, at the end of the day, I know that's on me."
~Director

This may sound random, but how would you describe a castle? What words immediately come to mind? Would you say it is a fluid structure, continuously in flux, and every day it is a surprise to wake up and see if it is still standing? No, not likely, unless you are describing a sand castle!

You probably would be more inclined to say a castle is a formidable structure, embodying stability, because people trust it is consistent, predictable, solid, and strong. Imagine how unsettling it would be for people in the kingdom where the castle was located, if every day they awoke to unexpected (significant or minor) changes in the castle! What feelings would that evoke? What impact would that have? Would the element of the unexpected/unpredictable chip away at their feelings of stability? Would it make people question the leadership, or contribute to people having fears, insecurities, and an overall lack of trust? Would it inevitably cause people to question the viability of the kingdom?

Chances are the ongoing unpredictability would wreak havoc, on every level, with the entire community.

Castles are meant to be solid, predictable, and capable of withstanding the test of time. This is important because people do best when they have a literal or figurative structure they can rely on, trust, and expect. This does not mean change and growth cannot happen, it simply means when it does happen it is part of a thoughtful and intentional process, with communication and involvement of all impacted parties.

Now think about your workplace, and the environment you have created for your team, through this lens. Have you built a Castle of Consistency around norms/expectations and overall structure? Are things clear, defined, and consistent? Can people trust that there is order and reliability to the content and the process of their work? Can workers know, understand and rely on your procedures, protocols, structures, infrastructure, and overall "norms?" Does the team have faith there is space, a place, and a purpose for them?

A Castle of Consistency is focused on building stable norms/ expectations within a team. It's about building a climate and culture based on fairness, equality, and stability that people can consistently predict and expect. It is about ensuring that you have created something solid and stable, embodying power and trust.

Would you say your team culture/climate is solid, like a castle? Or does your culture/climate reflect of the stress/anxiety that accompanies pervasive unpredictability? How does this Castle of Consistency transfer to your world?

> You might want to explore building a Castle of Consistency if, when reflecting on any of your past actions, behaviors, or decisions, your replies include any combination of the following:
>
> >> "Well, I don't usually do that, but..."
> >> "I know this isn't how we typically do things, but..."
> >> "No, I would never do that, unless..."
> >> "I wouldn't normally say that, but..."
> >> "I know I did that (said that, emailed that). I typically wouldn't do that, except ..."
> >> "I know how it looks (or sounds), but..."
> >> "That's rarely done, but in this particular case..."

Have you ever felt compelled to justify any of your actions with the replies above? You may have done/said it "but," as if the "but" would explain, rationalize, or validate why you changed the rules that time.

You are not alone. Those sentences have been used over and over, as people tried to explain why they did or didn't do something, and why the team should trust it won't happen again. "But" never qualifies, fixes, or eliminates anything. Remember how the book started? We already established they are watching everything you say and everything you do, all the time, which means even your best "but..." won't ever make it OK.

What does this mean?

As *The Dream Boss*, you must reject hypocrisy and all it stands for, embodies, and symbolizes. If everything you say and do sends a message, you know if it doesn't work for them, it can't work for you. You live by the same expectations, rules, standards, and structure that your team does. If your kid has a Little League game, that's important and it's great for you to go to it. Guess what? They have kids, too, and they'd love to "scoot out early" to catch the game. Or, maybe they don't have kids, but they have family and friends and things that mean a lot to them. If your schedule is flexible, in order to take into account your busy and important life, then theirs needs to be, as well.

Ultimately, any form of a double standard eats away at the foundational spirit of the team and takes away from your credibility. In every training, groups quickly name hypocrisy as one of the first examples of a bad supervisor. They fire off example after example, particularly around job performance, schedules, and accountability with time, of supervisors who operated by a different set of rules and adhered to a different set of standards from the rest of the team.

> ## If you are going to build a Castle of Consistency, remember the following:
>
> \>> If it applies or does not apply to you, then it applies or does not apply to everyone.
>
> \>> If there is an established policy/procedure/expectation, then it applies to all staff consistently, not just the ones you don't particularly like, or based on your mood that day.
>
> \>> Be hypersensitive to equality and how that plays out on your team. Know we all show up for it all, including you. It goes a long way for the team to see you pitching in, helping out, and participating.
>
> \>> If you are in charge, you have power. Power means people watch you. Power means people are acutely aware of your actions and highly sensitive to what you say/do with everyone, not just them. People will take notice and keep track.
>
> \>> Keep in mind when people are busy taking stock of not only where they stand with you, but also where others are at, it creates feelings of competition, frustration, drama, discord, discontent, pressure, anxiety, and agitation for your team, and for you. If these issues impact your team, it is important to look for the gaps, holes, and cracks in leadership.

When your team can trust there is a Castle of Consistency, they will trust you. They will trust that you are invested in keeping it equal, so they will trust you when you take action, even if that action is with them.

How can you work to build a solid and stable climate and culture to support the success of your team? The Castle of Consistency can be a helpful framework to explore where things are working, and where you may want to focus or expand your efforts.

Action: Castle of Consistency

Examine the messages you are sending to send to staff. Are the same norms/rules, expectations, and standards consistently applied to all staff? Do they also apply to you? Pay close attention to challenging/sensitive areas, or places where there may have been issues with the team in the past. Have you ever had issues due to inconsistencies? What happened, and why did it happen?

Past Issues: What went wrong?

Why did it happen?

Define: **WHAT**

What kind of solid, stable, strong environment do you want to create for your team? Specifically name policies, procedures, protocols, standards, norms, climate/culture expectations you will have for all team members, including yourself.

What is your specfic, concrete, and measurable goal? (How much, how many, and by when?)

What would having this mean to you, or do for you?

What is of value to you about this goal?

What does your goal look like when you've reached it, or how will you know you have reached it?

Clarify: WHY

Why is it important for you to create a solid, stable, strong environment? Why does it matter to you that the team feels like they are treated equally and that you are consistent and fair with everyone?

Why are you invested in reaching your goal?

Why do you feel a sense of passion, commitment, or alignment around this goal?

Why is this goal a priority for you?

Why would reaching this goal be of value to you, your work, or your life?

Implement: HOW

How will you make this happen? How will you make the changes necessary to create the workplace you described? How will you take action and include others in this initiative?

How will you develop a plan and timeline for reaching this goal?

How will you know you have achieved your goal?

How will you address any barriers, challenges, or obstacles?

How/ to whom will you be accountable?

3. Know the Goal to Win the Game: Power of Clear Expectations

"I think about my goals when they are bigger, like a large project or event, but not when I head in to meetings or supervision. I never thought about that before." ~Director

Before any meeting, conversation, interaction, or supervision, do you take a moment to get clear on what you hope to accomplish in the exchange? Do you have a clearly named and defined goal? Or, perhaps a better question would be, did you even know you should have a goal?! If you are like most people you are blazing from one meeting to the next, one conversation to the next, without a second to think about what you're trying to do (or get, or learn, or cover), never mind figure out whether or not you ever got it.

As a leader, a lot is missing if you are moving through your days with an overall absence of clarity. It's absolutely absurd to think that you could ever end your day thinking about the accomplishments and successes if you've never taken the time to name what an accomplishment or success would even look like!

Here's another way to think about this: If you headed out onto the field and saw a pile of sports equipment and were told to "go win the game," you would be confused. People want you to win, and you certainly want to win, but what should you do? Should you kick a ball, throw a ball, hit a puck, or make a basket? Are you playing alone, with a team, or with a partner? Obviously you want to do your best, and do what's right, but what are you trying to do? How could you ever strategize a plan to win if you never identified what you're trying to accomplish?

You could be thinking, "Well, that's just absurd! Of course I wouldn't make any moves on the field or the court until I knew what I was trying to do!" That is logical. Nobody would make a move until they knew what the goal was, but can this strategy apply once we leave the equipment behind and head in to the office?

Can you imagine the impact of having clear goals, objectives, and expectations in the office? Take a minute and imagine what would happen in your managing/supervising, or meetings, trainings, or conference calls, if you took a minute before you started to get clear and asked yourself, "What is my goal in this situation? What am I trying to do?" There is no doubt the workplace would be vastly different if people spent more time on the front end getting clear on goals, so they could spend less time on the back end doing damage control and putting out fires.

The power of clarity gives you the pause you need be in control of your thoughts and actions. It gives you the power that comes with focus and helps to shift your mood, direct your energy, and set your intention. It increases the likelihood that you will achieve your goal and meet your objective. It makes you thoughtful and clear. Bottom line, taking a minute to name your goal will put you ahead of the masses, since this is something that nobody seems to be doing, as evidenced by the amount of energy people spend on damage control at work.

If you walk on the field or court, you won't start playing full force until you know what the goal is, because you know you want to do your best. Implement that same level of clarity and focus as a manager in all of your interactions with the team. When you do, take notice of how powerful you feel, how other people respond to that power, and the endless number of "wins" filling your days!

Action: Know the Goal to Win the Game

Think about interactions with members of your team (meetings/supervision/training, etc.)

> How have you prepared for meetings/supervision, etc., in the past?

How has it worked for you?

Can you think about times you did not have a goal, and how that impacted the exchange?

Define: WHAT

What goals do you want to set around your interactions, meetings, supervisions, etc.? What kind of "win" would you get from setting goals?

> **What is your specific, concrete, and measurable goal? (How much, how many, by when?)**

> **What would having this mean to you, or do for you?**

> **What is of value to you about this goal?**

> **What does your goal look like when you've reached it, or how will you know when you have reached it?**

Clarify: WHY

Why is it important to you to have goals before you enter in to a conversation or meeting? Why will you/your team benefit from this level of goal setting and intentional clarity?

Why are you invested in reaching your goal?

Why do you feel a sense of passion, commitment, or alignment around this goal?

Why is this goal a priority for you?

Why would reaching this goal be of value to you, your work, or your life?

Implement: HOW

How will you start to apply the strategies of Know the Goal to Win the Game in your daily interactions with your team?

How will you develop a plan and timeline for reaching this goal?

How will you know you have achieved your goal?

How will you address any barriers, challenges, or obstacles?

How/ to whom will you be accountable?

4. Communicate to Completion: Power of Effective Communication

"A simple communication exchange didn't go well and it cost this department countless staff hours and thousands of dollars. People say they don't have time (to communicate well), and I'm going to say that you better make the time. I certainly won't make that mistake again!"   ~Manager

Most people spend a significant portion of each day in some kind of state of communication, meaning every day we are all involved in countless communication exchanges. Some exchanges are benign, with minor or minimal impact on our lives if they don't go well, while others are quite significant, with the potential for extensive trauma or drama if there is a communication miss. With all the communication we are engaged in, it may come as a surprise to learn that most of our communication would actually be considered partial or incomplete communication.

What constitutes partial or incomplete communication? It means after we say, type, or text our message, whatever our message may be, then we consider the exchange done. We literally or figuratively walk away. We assume that we clearly said it, so they must have understood what we meant and what we want/need them to do with our message. If we bother to take the time to ask the other person if they "got it," and they nod or mumble, "yeah," then we are absolutely certain it was a success. We had something to say, we said it nice and clear, and we feel pretty good about doing our part. If there is any confusion, or if the communication goes tragically awry, then it is obviously something to be owned by the other party.

You may have noticed there are a lot of people walking around proudly proclaiming themselves great communicators. Unfortunately for many of us, the reality is a significant portion of our daily communication is unsuccessful. In fact, because so many times it is not successful, it actually feels like divine intervention when it really does work. Effective and successful communication doesn't have to be a big mystery or an ongoing game of hit or miss. Would you be interested to know there is one thing you can do to dramatically increase your communication success rate, reduce conflict, build relationships, and expand productivity?

Most leaders are very, very interested in learning about what they can do to increase successful communication. Here it is: The missing link in communication is found in moving the finish line with your communication exchange, because communication doesn't end when you're done with your message. Your communication is only complete when you have confirmation that the other person has both heard and understood your message. This is the single most important thing you can do to alleviate misunderstandings, reduce conflict, and minimize drama.

When you communicate to completion, you're making sure there is feedback coming back to you about what this person understands, or will do, or will make happen. Another way to think about it is, you aren't done after you throw the ball, because you have to make sure someone caught it. The same principle applies here. This is a significant shift for people and takes practice and commitment to consistently apply the strategy, but it works. If you use it, it will unequivocally work—with an almost-foolproof success rate.

Almost all conflict comes from a communication breakdown. It's not with mal-intent that things unravel, and it's not because people enjoy conflict. It's most often because there was a communication "miss." Communication is not a seamless process, because we all don't share a brain, or universal frame of reference, or a standardized database of implicit/explicit meaning. We are all different, and therefore ascribe meaning differently to every level of our experience, understanding, and interpretation of communication. It is imperative for you to take time to make sure that people understand what you're saying, especially as a leader. When you are in charge, it's crucial for you to foster and maintain a climate committed to clear, effective, and productive communication.

As supervisors, we hit the ground running and assume people are with us. We think they get it, and they're clear. Sometimes we say some version of "so, you understand?" or maybe, "are we clear on this?" or perhaps we just say, "Got it?" To which the employee always says, "Yup!" Off you both go, only to find out next Tuesday, when the report is due, that they actually did not understand what you meant at all. Or maybe you find out when they don't show up for the shift that was changed. Or perhaps it becomes evident when there is a crisis exploding on a Friday afternoon and you realize that the message you thought they understood wasn't clear after all. That misconstrued memo dances to the tune of 127 hours of staff time to rectify, translating to thousands of wasted dollars and many sleepless nights on your end.

How do you close the communication loop? Quite simply, you ask for feedback. You need to know before the meeting/ supervision/training/conversation is over, what did the employee understand? What did they "get" from that exchange?

What will they do? What will happen? When will it happen? How will there be follow up or check-in's? It's not in a condescending or micromanaging way ("What did I just say? Repeat it back."). It's more in the spirit of, "Let's recap, and as we wrap up, make sure we're all on the same page. What's happening next? What are you doing, and how will we follow up?"

This is actually a great conversation to have as a larger group, because it helps people establish a new shared norm around communication. It's not the responsibility of one person in a communication exchange to make sure this happens. It's on both ends, so whether you're saying it, or it's being said to you, there should be a closing summary before walking away. People like to assume if there is any miscommunication that it was on the other party, because it certainly couldn't be that their initial message was unclear. On the other hand, people also assume if someone says something unclear to them, then it's not their problem if they didn't get it. Unfortunately the clarity of any message, in any exchange, is on both parties to own. Shifting an understanding of shared accountability to both parties helps increase the chances of successfully closing the communication loop.

It's important to emphasize that both parties are accountable. That means even if you didn't want to be involved, didn't like the content, didn't understand the purpose, or didn't have interest in any of the material shared, if someone says something to you, you are both in it now. Whether you said it, or it's said to you, be professional and make sure that you're clear before you walk away. The exchange isn't over until things have been clarified and confirmed. It's on both of you to make it work, because it will be on both of you if or when it doesn't! It's amazing how well this tool works, if you take the time to actually do it.

Action: Communicate to Completion

Think about your communication with your team. Where is it successful and where do you think it can it be improved?

Has there ever been a time when communication did not go the way you wanted, or was not clear, or successful, or effective? What happened? Where was the breakdown? Would this situation have turned out differently if you had asked for feedback on the front end?

Define: WHAT

What is your communication goal? What will you do to make sure you communicate to completion? What settings/situations do you want to focus on?

What is your specific, concrete, and measurable goal? (How much, how many, by when?)

What would having this mean to you, or do for you?

What is of value to you about this goal?

What does your goal look like when you've reached it, or how will you know when you have reached it?

Clarify: **WHY**

Why is it important for you to communicate effectively?

Why are you invested in reaching your goal?

Why do you feel a sense of passion, commitment, or alignment around this goal?

Why is this goal a priority for you?

Why would reaching this goal be of value to you, your work, or your life?

Implement: HOW

How will you develop a concrete action plan on your new communication strategy?

> **How will you develop a plan and timeline for reaching this goal?**

> **How will you know you have achieved your goal?**

> **How will you address any barriers, challenges, or obstacles?**

> **How/ to whom will you be accountable?**

7 POSITIVE

*"It's only a thought
and a thought can be changed."*
~Louise Hay

The positive is an energy boost and the negative is an energy drain.

Read that one again. A simple sentence with the capacity to be a catalyst to shift how you move through the world.

If you apply that concept, what are the implications for you, your team, your work? Understanding the far-reaching impact of what that implies, on all levels, could be the biggest motivation for every leader out there to figure out ways to capitalize on the positive. If the positive is an energy boost, how does this increased energy impact a team? What is the impact on motivation? Morale? Investment? Productivity? Relationships and workplace dynamics? Play it out. What happens to a team, department, agency, business, or bottom line when all of those areas have an infusion of energy? As a leader you know a lot happens, and all of it is good.

Understanding that a climate/culture focused on the positive creates energy, which benefits so many layers of the workplace, it suddenly makes the positive a high priority for leaders. Even leaders that aren't interested in traditional or typical "feel good" strategies suddenly begin paying attention to this connection to energy, because more energy leads to more of every-thing. More productivity. More success. More growth. More movement. More investment. More participation. More excitement. More alliance from staff. More money. Have you ever heard a leader say that they didn't care about those things? The universal goals of every great leader are to inspire a team to achieve "more," on every level.

The infusion of energy that accompanies the positive is just as strong in the other direction when you flip to the negative. The negative is the greatest energy drain any leader will know. A focus on the negative translates to a workplace void of energy, spark, passion, or motivation. People aren't connected, and because of that lack of connection, the team isn't doing much, and what they are doing, they're not doing very well. The negative can actually lead to "more" as well, but it's more of all of the things you don't want. More apathy, more ambivalence, and more conflict. The negative breeds more struggles, a deeper lack of trust, and high turnover. Clearly, the negative is toxic, so it is safe to assume if you are leading a group you are invested in the positive because there is a big payoff for you, your team, and the bottom line.

For many people, finding and naming the positive in the world is a significant shift from the traditional focus they grew up with, which is typically centered on what went wrong. In many, many ways we are a deficit-based culture. We are skilled at noticing and naming what we don't like and we always make time to share negative experiences. We are taught to address what is wrong, what isn't working, what didn't get done, didn't go well, didn't happen, or didn't make us happy. People will tell you how busy they are, yet in the midst of their busy lives, they somehow always manage to find time to complain.

We feel comfortable finding managers in stores and restaurants to make sure they are aware of the rude employee, cold chicken, or dirty glass on the table. We ask to see the manager whenever our feathers are ruffled, and all managers know it. Watch their body language as you approach; it's as if they are bracing themselves for the expected torrent of hostility and anger the public regularly bestows on them. If someone wants to talk to them, then chances are inordinately high it will be about something wrong. It's unfortunate we are so predictable.

We complain in person, on the phone, online, and through social networks. Many of us are proficient at finding, naming, and sharing our dissatisfaction, and take great pride in making the world aware of it. Notice how many people in social settings solely focus on the litany of negative experiences they have endured. They cover all that is wrong when out to lunch, out with friends, over dinner, on a Friday night, or away on vacation. It's all about what went wrong, or who did something wrong. The focus on the negative is significant because it impacts a person's mood, outlook, feelings, and beliefs. Take note of how negative people report feeling physically and you don't need to be a doctor to observe some interesting patterns. Turns out on every level, mentally, emotionally, and physically, it literally feels bad to be grounded in the negative.

If the negative has such a profound impact on our thoughts, feelings, attitudes, moods, and overall outlook, what does that mean about the positive? It means exactly the same thing, except the positive has a significant impact in the other direction. It feels good to look for and name what is right with people, experiences, and the world. Mentally, physically, and emotionally there is a tremendous value in finding and focusing on the positive. The powerful impact of the positive focus permeates mood, outlook, feelings, and beliefs, and serves as a catalyst to shift one's entire experience of life. After working with thousands of people, of all ages, there has never been an example of too much positive in someone's life! This is a skill everyone could benefit from developing further.

How can you expand your capacity to find and name the positive, not just at work, but in your world? It's how you move through your days, every day, and what lens you use to filter your experiences. Have you ever called over the manager to appreciate, notice, and acknowledge a fabulous experience at a store or restaurant? Have you written a letter, made a phone call, tweeted or Facebooked about a positive experience, interaction, or exchange? "Why, yes I have!" some of you may say with glee, and proceed to point out a time, six years ago, when you did just that. Many have said they "thought about it" or "wanted to" but they didn't. It's great that it crossed your mind, or that you actually did it once or twice, but imagine making it part of your day, every day?

What would the impact be if you made the positive a foundational part of your world? Could you build in a plan to actively seek out the positive, the successes, and the great moments that deserve a spotlight of recognition and appreciation? Another angle could be, if you were to receive a cash bonus every time you found and named a positive in your world, what would the result be? You would be a millionaire, wouldn't you? You would look for the positive, find it everywhere, name it proudly, and celebrate it with glee! The positive is everywhere, and it is begging for you to take notice of it. You won't be getting cash, but you will be getting something incredibly valuable for your efforts. Your whole life experience, at work and in the world, benefits from this new positive lens.

As a leader, can you model what it looks like to move through this world with a tilt toward the positive? The benefits are endless, for you, your team, and the work you all do together.

Action: Assessing the Positive

Do you look for and find the positive in people, performances, and projects? Think about how you find and name the positive in your life.

> Where do you, or could you, find, name, and celebrate the positive ...

> About you?

> At work?

> In your world?

Hint: Think about what is working, succeeding, what you appreciate, what you feel grateful for, what you love, what you value, what brings you joy/peace/contentment in the areas above. Notice how you feel when you focus on the positive. It shifts your energy, alters your mood, and fundamentally shifts your world view. The positive is powerful, so use it!

If you are wondering, "What does this have to do with being the boss?" It has everything to do with it! If your lens is focused only on pointing out/noticing the negative, that transfers to work. If you move through your days missing what went well, because you are focused on finding and addressing what did not go well, that transfers to work. Maybe you are someone that doesn't point out the negative or the positive, because you can't be bothered with any of it. That will come across at work as well.

As a leader it is important for you to be dialed in to the impact your focus and energy, positive or negative, has on your team. It is also key for you to understand if you choose to consistently and consciously focus on the positive, there is an immediate benefit to your team. People quickly learn you are a leader who takes notice of the positive. You not only notice the positive, you recognize it, and you celebrate it! As managers/supervisors, we often forget we make an incredible impact on people by what we say, or don't say, and by what we do, or don't do. There are a lot of leaders choosing to make that impact a positive one, and it is making a difference in so many lives.

Here are four tools/strategies to help you become a more Positive leader:

1. The Positive Promise: Change Your Lens, Change Your World

I know I do better, and I feel better, when my attention on the positive, but I honestly don't always think about that angle when working with my team."
~Team Leader

How can you check to see if things are focused on the positive at work? It's important to assess overall policies, norms, structure, and language. Think about meetings, projects, evaluations, and supervision. Where is the spotlight? It is on what is right and what is working? Is it on highlights, successes, and growth? Is it about validation, recognition, and appreciation? Or is your typical focus centered on what went wrong?

It is fascinating to see how many people have meetings, training, and supervision to primarily focus on or process what didn't happen, didn't get done, didn't go well, or didn't work. It's not a bad thing to explore what went awry, because it's necessary to learn and grow, but shining the light on the negative doesn't typically serve as a catalyst to launch people forward. Remember, the negative is an energy drain. Often people focus on all the problems, deplete the collective energy tank to zero, then ask the group to come up with excited, inspired, innovative ideas to address the issues and solve the problems. They seem puzzled and befuddled to find the team flat, disconnected, disinterested, and disengaged.

It's fascinating to watch because once the negative is addressed, and the room is filled with people in an apathetic and uninspired state, they then ask the group, "So people, what can we do differently next time? How can you make this better, or make sure that what went wrong won't go wrong again?" What do you think happens then? Exactly. Nothing! There aren't any new angles or new ideas because the energy has been drained! So many people regularly do this. Maybe you are realizing you have even done it in the past with your team. Is it a surprise to see people don't have energy or excitement after they've been drowning in what went wrong and where they failed?

If you want people to be engaged, invested, excited, and fully participate as they collectively plan out how to go to the next level, ask them where they have succeeded, and how they plan on doing, being, or achieving more as they go forward.

You want to see a group explode? Focus on the positive, what is amazing, and what they are excited about. Feel the energy soar, and then from that place, ask the group where they can grow/expand/improve. They will innately address all of the missing pieces, broken parts, and unconnected dots as they eagerly plan next steps. The ownership, investment, and excitement is magical. Using this approach to of group facilitation clearly makes sense, yet it's amazing to see how new it is for so many leaders.

As you apply this concept to your team in a concrete way, what could it look like? You could start the team meeting/supervision with some kind of combination of, "Let's look at what worked. Where did we hit it out of the park? Where were you impressed with how we did? What were some of the highlights? Where do you feel you were successful?" This gets the energy up. This makes people feel good, as it should, and serves to shine the light on what worked and what went well.

Next, ask what they could do to make it better, enhance it, expand it, or improve it for next time. Smiling and sparkling, they will tell you individually what they can and will do to make it better, as well as how they will work together to improve things in the future. When you focus on the positive, it works wonders, but when your team focuses on the positive, it is magic.

In order for a leader to focus on the positive, it requires you to have some level of investment in finding the positive. You can't focus on something you don't see. The Positive Promise is a tool to help people see the steps they can take to build a solid, positive foundation. The Positive Promise works because it is simple; easy to understand, easy to remember, and easy to use.

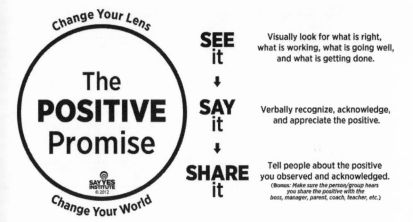

The first step is to notice the positive, but after you see it, what else can you do with it? Can you say something to directly acknowledge the positive experience, action, event, or exchange to the person/ group responsible for it? You would feel good, because it feels great to shine a spotlight on the positive, but they would feel great, too! What if you took it one level higher and you shared the positive experience you observed with other people? Do you see how powerful positive energy can be, and just like everything, how it exponentially grows the more attention it receives?

The Positive Promise is a model every leader would benefit from using on a regular basis, as it serves as a reminder the focus of the leader matters, and there can never be too much positive in the world, or at work.

Action: The Positive Promise

If the positive is an energy boost and the negative is an energy drain, it's helpful to take inventory on your focus and your energy at work.

Where has your focus/energy been?

Where do you want it to be?

How do you/ can you use the positive with your team?

Define: WHAT

What type of workplace do you want to create and maintain? What do you want it to look like, be like, feel like? What will you choose to focus on? How will your focus contribute to building a positive environment?

> **What is your specific, concrete, and measurable goal? (How much, how many, by when?)**

> **What would having this mean to you, or do for you?**

> **What is of value to you about this goal?**

> **What does your goal look like when you've reached it, or how will you know when you have reached it?**

Clarify: **WHY**

Why is it important for you to focus on building the positive? Why are you interested in the impact the positive could have on the team?

Why are you invested in reaching your goal?

Why do you feel a sense of passion, commitment, or alignment around this goal?

Why is this goal a priority for you?

Why would reaching this goal be of value to you, your work, or your life?

Implement: HOW

How will you take action steps to direct your focus and your energy to the positive in your daily world? How will you do things differently around noticing and acknowledging the positive?

How will you develop a plan and timeline for reaching this goal?

How will you know you have achieved your goal?

How will you address any barriers, challenges, or obstacles?

How/ to whom will you be accountable?

2. Fill Your Well: You can't give what you don't have!

"I am stressed and overwhelmed and feel like I'm running on empty. It's like I have nothing left to give staff. I know they need more from me, but I just don't have it in me."
~ Manager

We have established it matters if the leader is positive, and makes a significant impact on the whole team when a leader can see, and name, what is working. We are covering how to be positive in the world and positive with your staff/team. We are exploring how you can fully own the power that comes with being positive, and how you can use that power to shift how you move through you daily life. At this point, you are on board and feeling excited about fully embracing your newfound passion for all things positive, except under that enthusiasm is a little bit of doubt, because you are silently wondering who can actually maintain this state in daily life or in the "real world."

Being positive can feel like a lot of work, and some complain it is too hard to see what's right, when it's clear so much is wrong. Who are these people who can consistently embrace the upside of people, experiences, and life? Positive people are not living perfect lives, filled with endless moments of unadulterated bliss. These are not people dealt a better hand in life, or simpletons living simple lives devoid of any struggles, challenges, trauma, or drama. Positive people are living the same diverse life experiences as everyone else, yet they somehow manage to feel varying degrees of positive emotions on a regular and consistent basis. They are often described as being strong, happy, fulfilled, content, peaceful, calm, healthy, connected, joyful, optimistic, energetic, engaged, loving, grateful, and present. They aren't living perfect lives, but they do a great job finding and focusing on what is right, even when some things may be wrong.

It's almost as if positive people share so much or give so much because they have so much inside to draw on, enabling them to see the world and the people in it in a more positive light. What does this have to do with managing people? You cannot give what you do not have. If you are running on empty and living in a depleted, burnt out, exhausted, stressed, overwhelmed, overloaded, and drained state, then you are not in a position to be harnessing the power of the positive with your team. You will not see what is right, what is going well, and what is getting done if you have nothing inside. Why? Because you simply cannot get water from an empty, dry well.

Let's talk about wells. How does a well work? A well consistently gives out water because it is designed with a continuous supply of water coming in to the well, so there can be a continuous supply of water going out of the well. In one respect we are a lot like a well; we continuously give a lot, day in and day out. Unfortunately we are missing the other crucial piece of the well, as people do not have a continuous source of refueling, refilling, replenishing happening in their daily lives. After asking countless people, "what fills your well?" it became tragically clear we have a lot of empty, dry, and dusty wells out there!

Your Life Well was created to help people visually grasp the importance of making time for what refuels, refills, or replenishes them, or else the well runs dry. This model is not something specific to one type of person, or one kind of industry. This tool can be universally applied and the goal is to help people look at self care through a different lens.

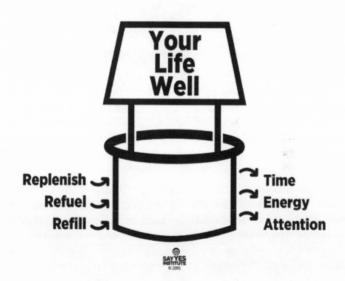

Action: Take inventory of *Your Life Well*

>> **Step 1:** Draw *Your Life Well* on a piece of paper.

>> **Step 2:** What is taking your time/energy/attention? Draw arrows and name those things taking energy OUT of *Your Life Well*. This is for you to get a sense of where you spend your time, energy, and attention. It should help you grasp the range and scope of what you are putting out every day.

>> **Step 3:** What replenishes, refuels, and refills you? Draw arrows coming IN to *Your Life Well* and name what nourishes you. These are not things that require a lot of time or money (a vacation next year doesn't count!); these are things you can do every day. You may not necessarily be doing them all right now, but it's important for you to know what they are. Can you come up with at least 10 things with the ability to fill *Your Life Well*?

>> **Step 4:** Take inventory of what is going out and what is coming in. Are you doing enough to take care of yourself? When looking at *Your Life Well*, most people find they need to do more to replenish, refuel, and refill the well. Can you commit to doing more of the things that refill *Your Life Well*? What will you do within the next day? How will you keep filling *Your Life Well* on a daily basis?

People often say they simply "don't have time" to do anything to refill their well. They are busy, important people who do a lot, give a lot, are responsible for a lot, manage a lot, produce a lot, etc., and they just can't spare a minute to do anything they view as being optional or elective. There is nothing optional or elective about filling one's well. When people do not take care of themselves, and the well runs dry, the impact is significant.

When clients come in to coaching it is often with lists of perceived "problem areas" in life where they are struggling, and it quickly becomes clear for the majority of the people it comes down to an empty well. They are burnt out, stressed, exhausted, overwhelmed, overloaded, depressed, or empty. They share examples of struggles with family, friends, work, and their health. Whatever examples or descriptions they give, the bottom line seems to always land with the reality they haven't been taking care of themselves. People are often struck by how little comes in to their well, because they haven't made it a priority. If you are giving a lot every day, then you need daily filling. People, including managers and supervisors, are at their best when the well is full, or at least has a steady supply of some water coming in to it!

Your Life Well is important because everything you want to do, achieve, or accomplish as a leader starts with you. You bring you into the office every day, thereby making you and how you feel a foundational part of this process. Again, you can't give what you don't have. As a leader it takes a lot of energy to focus on the positive, communicate effectively, support professional growth, maintain accountability, and hold the larger vision for the team. In order to do all of this, you must take care of you. That's the only way to do it, because that's the only way you can do it. In order to give a lot, you need to have a lot to give, so make sure you are filling *Your Life Well*!

Action: Fill Your Well

Take inventory of how you are feeling right now. Think about your physical state, in addition to your mental/ emotional state.

In general, would you say you feel calm, focused, peaceful, powerful, positive, and in a good place with things? If that is not an accurate description, then how do you feel? Think about your work world, then go macro and think about your entire world. What words accurately capture how you feel?

Define: WHAT

What did you notice about how you feel and the connection to *Your Life Well*? What are you currently doing to take care of yourself, so you have energy to bring to your team (and your life)? What do you want to do more of?

What is your specific, concrete, and measurable goal? (How much, how many, by when?)

What would having this mean to you, or do for you?

What is of value to you about this goal?

What does your goal look like when you've reached it, or how will you know when you have reached it?

Clarify: WHY

Why is it important for you to spend time/energy on filling your well?

Why are you invested in reaching your goal?

Why do you feel a sense of passion, commitment, or alignment around this goal?

Why is this goal a priority for you?

Why would reaching this goal be of value to you, your work, or your life?

Implement: HOW

How will you take steps to start filling your well? How will you do things differently?

How will you develop a plan and timeline for reaching this goal?

How will you know you have achieved this goal?

How will you address any barriers, challenges, or obstacles?

How/ to whom will you be accountable?

3. Mental Ticker Tape: Owning Your Thoughts

"I know it's important to be positive, and I think I'm saying the right things, but if people could see what I was thinking they would be horrified! If I had to be honest, I'm not really that optimistic about whether or not we can really do this (make changes)."

~Director

A lot of people say they work really hard to be positive, and find what is right, what is working, and what is going well. They want to stay in the place where they can capitalize on the immense power that comes with positive energy. Every day they want to do it, yet there are things getting in the way making it difficult for people to stay in that place.

Do you know what the most common struggle is for people? It's something most people don't even know is happening, so they have no ability to address it. It's the mental ticker tape running nonstop in your head, and it's typically programmed with negative sentiments. Sentiments so negative it could appear as if it were operated by some kind of pessimistic, evil, horrid creature with the sole purpose of sabotaging your world because it negatively targets anyone, everyone, and anything in your life.

For many people the Mental Ticker Tape is a new concept. Do you know what a ticker tape is? It's typically a black sign, with red writing running across the screen, telling you how much milk is, or what's on sale, or shares some kind of message/greeting or update. It simply runs the same message over and over, until someone changes the content. Do you have a visual?

Imagine that you have one of those in your head, which runs all day long with countless messages about your world and the people in it. This is not a phenomenon unique to you, as we all have it, and it's always running. We just aren't conscious of it, so we never examine the content for accuracy, meaning, or impact.

If you are in doubt that this applies to you, or questioning if you have an active Mental Ticker Tape, see if any of this rings a bell …

> **You say:** "Sally, I'm really excited to meet with you later. I'm looking forward to reading your report!"

> **Mental Ticker Tape:** *Right. As if that will be done, since you never finish anything on time. I bet you haven't even started.*

You say: "This team is really working hard and we're on track to meet our goals. You should be proud!"

Mental Ticker Tape: *Who are we kidding? Most of you did nothing. Good thing Claire and Tyson carried the ball for you all. Again. This team is a joke.*

Actually, you don't even say anything out loud; you could just think it, because the Mental Ticker Tape is just as proficient at responding to solely internal thoughts. So proficient you never even know it is happening. Did you know the Mental Ticker Tape doesn't just run negative mental or verbal thoughts about other people? It actually runs endless streams of critical, negative, and less-than-kind statements about you, too! Here is another angle on the Mental Ticker Tape:

You think: "I'm going to work with the team on communication skills. I'll do training with them on it next week. That would be so helpful."

Mental Ticker Tape: *Train? What?! You can't train! Last training you did was awful. What are you thinking? You're no good at training. What a stupid idea!*

You think: "I'm going to ask for a raise. I work hard and I deserve it."

Mental Ticker Tape: *You're not getting a raise, so don't even bother. What have you even done this year? Forget it. You're not that good at what you do and they aren't giving you a dime more than you're getting, so stop dreaming. There isn't any money right now anyway, so it won't happen.*

Now let's take it out of the workplace, just to illustrate how this Mental Ticker Tape has the ability to permeate all parts of your life.

You think: "I'm going to just go over and ask him/her out. I'm going to just go do it. Why not, what can I lose?"

Mental Ticker Tape: *He/she will never go out with you. Look at you. You're a mess. You can't just walk up to someone like that because you look desperate. Nobody really does that. I bet they're already taken, anyway.*

You think: "I'm going to get healthy. I'm joining a gym and I'm going to eat better."

Mental Ticker Tape: *You aren't going to go to a gym! You never follow through on anything you start. You can buy fruit, but you won't eat it. You never do. You fail at this every time—so why even bother? It's pointless and you'll never do it. You're lazy. Don't waste your money on a lost cause.*

Does any of that sound familiar? Change the context, the players, the details, and could those read like they were lifted right out of your head? What is most concerning is this Mental Ticker Tape is actually not being run by some kind of evil creature, set on ensuring your demise. What makes this so bizarre is the ticker tape is solely run and staffed, around the clock, by you. Everything on it, every day, is what you put there. This is always a fun activity in trainings because people are really mystified as to how this could have happened, and continues to happen, without their knowledge or consent.

If you want to stay positive, it's imperative that you are in charge of what you are saying, and thinking, on a conscious and subconscious level. This means you are taking control of the conscious and intentional words you speak, as well as the subconscious and hidden beliefs you hold. Your Mental Ticker Tape can serve to be your greatest ally, supporting your positive thoughts, feelings, and actions, or it can be the biggest contributor in your self-sabotage. For most people just the awareness that they are running a Mental Ticker Tape is enough of a catalyst to shift the content to a more positive and productive flow.

Action: Control Your Mental Ticker Tape

You have a ticker tape running in your head all the time. It has thoughts about you, your abilities, your performance, your value/worth, etc., and it also has thoughts about everyone else around you. Are you aware of what your Mental Ticker Tape is saying?

Take inventory to determine if the messages you are putting on your Mental Ticker Tape are contributing to your life, at home and at work? Assess the content you are running on your Mental Ticker Tape and decide if those messages are positively or negatively impacting your world.

Define: WHAT

What messages do you want your ticker tape to say, about you and about the people in your world?

What is your specific, concrete, and measurable goal? (How much, how many, by when?)

What would having this mean to you, or do for you?

What is of value to you about this goal?

What does your goal look like when you've reached it, or how will you know when you have reached it?

Clarify: WHY

Why is it important for you to take ownership of the content of your ticker tape?

Why are you invested in reaching your goal?

Why do you feel a sense of passion, commitment, or alignment around this goal?

Why is this goal a priority for you?

Why would reaching this goal be of value to you, your work, or your life?

Implement: HOW

How will you take ownership of the messages/content of your ticker tape?
How will you take steps to change the content of your Mental Ticker Tape
and run messages that positively contribute to your overall mood/state/
outlook/perspective?

How will you develop a plan and timeline for reaching
this goal?

How will you know you have achieved this goal?

How will you address any barriers, challenges, or obstacles?

How/ to whom will you be accountable?

4. Other People's Stuff (OPS): The Power of Ownership

"I can't tell you how many days I leave here feeling like they're in competition for who has the biggest crisis happening in their lives. Everyone has a reason why they can't do something, or didn't get something done. I'm so tired of it falling on me to do it all."   ~Supervisor

Do you want to know what powerful people know? Do you want to know how they are able to maintain a powerful state, on a day to day basis? Not a lot of people know this one, so pay attention.

They don't carry Other People's Stuff (OPS).

They don't carry, internalize, personalize, own, or take on other people's issues, moods, struggles, challenges, problems, attitudes, hurts, frustrations, or anger. They move through the day able to simultaneously hold compassion for other people, while balancing an awareness that they are never responsible for fixing, curing, solving, rectifying, holding, owning, moving, or carrying anyone else's baggage. They refuse to be responsible for carrying Other People's Stuff.

This may sound like something everyone should already know and adhere to, but it's not. This concept is a mind-blowing new angle for a lot of people. It is important to note even those who already know about it are still guilty of regularly carrying other people's stuff.

The fact is, everyone has stuff. We all go through life carrying varying amounts of baggage from the past, as well as the continuous accumulation that comes from just living daily life. Side note: Some are so adept at this, they have even mastered the art of accumulating baggage from possible future actions or events they haven't even lived yet! The worry and anticipation of what could go wrong in the future has an amazing capacity to produce baggage at the same rate as experiences already lived. It is quite remarkable how many possible avenues one can accumulate stuff from. With so many equally accessible options to accumulate baggage, why does it seem some people have managed to collect and carry so much more than others?

Baggage is a given accompaniment of life, and showing up and moving through the world ensures you are going to be bumping in to a lot of moods, emotions, and attitudes. On a daily basis it takes a very clear and focused person to move through the world baggage free. Beyond the challenge of not accumulating your own baggage, from your own direct experiences, there are people out there actively looking to dump their "stuff" and give their baggage to other people. In other words, if they aren't ok, they want to make sure you aren't ok either. Then there are those people who seem to seek out other people's issues, problems, and struggles, and happily take them on as their own. Nobody asked them to take on drama, these people intentionally hunt it down and pick it up with glee. Any pain they can scoop up adds to their stockpile of misery, which they eagerly share with any and all in their path.

There are lots of ways to pick up baggage; inadvertently or willingly. People need to take inventory on what they are lugging around through life. The first step is to determine if what you are carrying is yours, or if it belongs to someone else. If it is yours, is carrying it adding anything to your life? Ask yourself if you want to continue carrying it. If you don't, let it go. If it's not yours, where did you get it, and why are you carrying it? What purpose does it serve if you continue to lug around other people's baggage? What benefits do you reap from carrying the anger, pain, frustration, or resentment from other people?

Part of being Powerful can transfer to a boss feeling a sense of responsibility or accountability for the struggles of people in his/her life. A lot of leaders are quick to take on a lot, or own a lot, which can morph in to them becoming a metaphorical dumping ground for the team, as well as other people in their lives. Holding and carrying excessive baggage leaves leaders feeling exhausted, depleted, stressed, frustrated, agitated, and overwhelmed.

I need to add something here, because in order to really get this activity, we need to get a little more graphic. What is another word for "stuff?"
You may say something like, baggage, luggage, crap, issues … But I'm looking for something crass and a term not really socially acceptable. Be really graphic.

S*#*.
Other People's "S*#%."
You know what I'm saying, right?

If you feel so inclined, wherever you see "stuff," please substitute the word "S#%*:" Why? Because in doing this training with thousands of people, it sig-

nificantly ramps up the impact of the activity and helps people see how freaky it is that so many of us willingly engage in such a horrifically inappropriate, unhealthy, and bizarre behavior, daily.

You would never walk in to a coffee shop, or a store, or a meeting, and then leave with bags of "S*%$" from other people, would you? That would be disgusting and obscene. Nobody would ever, ever, EVER do that. Yet we all do it every day with emotional baggage. Matter of fact, you have probably already done it many times today, and you just accept it as a normal part of life.

You do it.
Your team does it.
Your neighbors do it.
Your spouse does it.
Your sister does it.
Strangers do it.

If we aren't careful, or vigilant, it will happen countless times throughout the day, every day.

How do you know you are doing it? Someone else is angry and your chest constricts and blood pressure goes up. That means you just picked up a few of his/her "bags." You're in a meeting and you notice someone comes in agitated, and when the meeting's over now you are agitated, too. Good news, you just left with a bag or two. You enter a store happy, then after an unpleasant interaction with a cashier you leave the store with an edge or an attitude, you just left with someone else's baggage. See how fast it happens?

Here's how OPS works:
1. You are happy, content, fine, peaceful etc.
2. You encounter a person who is upset or angry, agitated, frustrated, stressed, etc.
3. You walk away and now you feel angry, agitated, frustrated, and stressed.

What happened? The person with the problem is gone, but the negativity is left behind. There you are, left holding his/her baggage, problems, anxieties, struggles, bad feelings, or bad moods. You are left with his/her "S*#&." The biggest piece is, you then carry it with you in to your day, from meeting to meeting, errand to errand, office to home. You move through your day, whether it's intentional or not, carrying OPS!

Here is a visual of what OPS looks like:

Other People's Stuff: OPS

A lot of us move through the world looking for, grabbing, picking up, and carrying OPS. As you move through the day you could start by transporting two bags, increase to 10 bags, then 23 bags, and end your day with 78 bags of OPS. Imagine transporting OPS with you throughout the day, and imagine it is exponentially increasing as the day goes on. How will this impact you? What does this do to your mood, your outlook, your energy, your state of mind?

Now, what does this mean if you're the boss? People are going to come in to work carrying a lot of "stuff." Whatever negativity, bad moods, frustrations, disappointments, failures, anger, or sadness people are carrying, it is ultimately on them to handle themselves appropriately at work. It's important to remember that even though people may be dealing with a lot, there is still an expectation if they show up for work, they will be able to work. They are being paid to do a job, and regardless of the baggage they are carrying, they are adults and it is reasonable to assume they will handle themselves in a professional manner. As the boss, you are there to encourage the professional growth and development of your team, not be a therapist or crisis counselor. You are there to support people, not fix people. You are there for your team, but you are not doing it for team. Be aware of how you support people, without taking on what isn't yours to carry, fix, deal with, or address.

How do you do this? You ask yourself some questions:
>> *How are you feeling?* Continuously check in with where you are at and how you feel before/after meetings, supervision, training, conversations etc. If you start out the day feeling pretty good, and end the day feeling like you've been steamrolled by life, it means during the day you were been very busy picking up and transporting OPS! Can you pinpoint where you seem to be picking up OPS? Most people have no idea how they are feeling, so they're oblivious as to how and when they got derailed.

>> *What are you going to do?* Once you notice you have been negatively impacted by someone else's mood and you are carrying around OPS, decide if it is helping you. Is it contributing to your day, your mood, your experience, or your life in a positive way? If it's not adding anything, do you want to keep doing it? What can you do differently going forward? Remember, if you don't have the power to control, or fix, or solve something, then it's not yours to carry!

How do you succeed with this one? It is imperative you are aware of what emotional state you're in and tune in to your thoughts/feelings on a regular basis. The reason most people succumb to carrying so much of OPS is because they are not paying attention to their moods/feelings. If you feel positive and you leave an interaction with a coworker/supervisee/family member/stranger and now you feel negative, agitated, or frustrated then it is possible you have just left with OPS. Was that your intention? Remember, if it isn't yours, it isn't yours to carry, so leave it behind!

Action: Drop Other People's Stuff (OPS)

Powerful people do not have time, space, or energy to carry Other People's Stuff. Think about your days at work and notice how you feel before, during, and after you meet with or interact with the team. Your mood is the best indicator of whether you're carrying anyone else's baggage, issues, struggles, frustrations, stressors, etc.

To help you clarify how you may be impacted by OPS, describe how you feel before, during, and after different meetings or exchanges. Do you notice any patterns?

Define: WHAT

What is your goal around carrying Other People's Stuff?

> **What is your specific, concrete, and measurable goal? (How much, how many, by when?)**

> **What would having this mean to you, or do for you?**

> **What is of value to you about this goal?**

> **What does your goal look like when you've reached it, or how will you know when you have reached it?**

Clarify: WHY

Why is it important for you to make changes around carrying Other People's Stuff?

> **Why are you invested in reaching your goal?**

> **Why do you feel a sense of passion, commitment, or alignment around this goal?**

> **Why is this goal a priority for you?**

> **Why would reaching this goal be of value to you, your work, or your life?**

Implement: HOW

How will you develop a plan to stop carrying Other People's Stuff? How will you leave meetings, supervisions, trainings, conference calls, etc., with no baggage? How can you support your team to understand and implement this tool as well?

How will you develop a plan and timeline for reaching this goal?

How will you know you have achieved this goal?

How will you address any barriers, challenges, or obstacles?

How/ to whom will you be accountable?

Footnote on OPS: The purpose of this tool is to give you a possible perspective to help you move through your day without taking on the moods, frustrations, issues, or stressors from other people. A lot of people find this to be a powerful tool to help them reframe ownership and accountability, yet many struggle with the perception this may in some way mean they don't care about the struggles/challenges or "stuff" someone else is carrying. That is not the case.

The purpose of OPS is to understand you cannot successfully take on, or take over, someone else's baggage. The only thing you can do, if it's appropriate, is support someone to recognize they are carrying baggage, and see if they think it makes sense for them to continue to do so. You can care about someone, but it's not up to you to fix, solve, or eliminate their struggles, pain, or difficulties. The hope is the OPS model will help people to understand the only person in a position to actually let go of baggage is the original owner.

8 PROFESSIONAL

"I praise loudly.
I blame softly."
~Catherine the Great

How important is it for a leader to be perceived as professional? Of the three components of this book, the professional piece could be the most interesting, because while not every leader confidently owns the identity of being powerful or positive, I have yet to meet a manager who did not claim to be professional. There appears to be a universal expectation or assumption that a leadership role implies one must innately embody what it means to be professional.

In countless workshops and trainings, "professional" is consistently one of the top words managers/ supervisors/leaders proudly used to describe who they are, or how they are. It is logical to assume a leader would consistently have the perception of being professional, simply based on the nature of the position, yet this is an area which is actually difficult for many people to master. It is not as easy, or as innate, as people expect it to be, and it is certainly not a way of being which automatically accompanies a title. This is a skill, and like all skills, only improves with time, energy, and attention.

To successfully own what it means to be professional it is imperative you are operating within an environment supporting a professional culture and climate. A professional environment reflects policies, procedures, and norms tied to the overall infrastructure, and encompasses evaluations, performance reviews, meetings, trainings, unrolling new initiatives, or anything else that frames the structure of how the team works, individually, collectively, and collaboratively.

If you are the leader, when you say something, or when you do something, make sure it is happening in a context that enables it to mean something.

"I don't know why they even bother—it's such a joke here. I do the yearly Employee Evaluation the week before it's due, and then we never look at it again, until next year."   ~Supervisor

"You have no idea how much I dread supervision. I don't do it often, but when I do it's painful for both of us."   ~Team Leader

"It feels like we follow a 'flavor of the month' kind of structure here. Every new training leads us in a new direction, so nobody seems too invested in any new ideas anymore and nothing we have tried has ever taken off."
                                                                      ~ Director

If you're going to continue doing things that don't mean anything, wouldn't it be freeing, and fun, to just call it what it is? It could sound something like this:

"We are about to embark on another round of evaluations. We all know that this is an arbitrary and superfluous process that has no merit and/or connection to your work, your salary or your performance. You and I will proceed with little thought and no pretense of investment as we try to piece together, based on sketchy memory, some semblance of your past year of performance, which will clearly rely heavily on the past two months, since that is all you and I are actually able to recall. We will then have an obligatory meeting, where we will both muddle through attempting to appear as though we both have some vested interest around this profoundly inadequate assessment of your performance and future potential. We will both watch the clock, knowing that in one short hour it will be over and we will sign the form and return it (filled with upcoming goals and perfunctory ramblings of successes/ challenges from the past year), to a file in a desk, where it shall remain safely undisturbed for the next 364 days. Please agree that you are complicit in this dirty little secret and we shall proceed, as planned, and as we have many times before. Thank you for your time."

How refreshing would it be to just call it what it is, which is nothing.

The tragedy in the scenario above is the possibility that it doesn't have to be. What if performance evaluations could be reclaimed as a useful process to guide professional growth and development? Unfortunately, for so many places, it is not used to its full potential and doesn't add anything to the culture. There are so many workplaces that have developed infrastructures that could provide valid, helpful, or powerful tools, but they simply aren't used properly or consistently.

Beyond evaluations, supervision is another area that consistently makes people cringe. So many supervisors and staff have repeatedly said, "What's the point of it? Why bother? It's a waste of time!"

It is a waste of time if it's sporadic, people are not prepared, or if there is no structure. It is a waste of time if it's merely a running report of what already was done, or consists of a supervisor rattling off a list of what tasks/projects need to be completed. If that's the case, why not just send a bulleted email and save you both that dreaded hour every week, or every month?

Supervision is an amazing opportunity to support staff development and growth. It is a chance for the supervisor to be pushed/challenged to find ways to support and motivate staff, while holding staff accountable for their professional performance and growth in a concrete and measurable way. There is immense power and possibility in the process of supervision, if you show up prepared and all parties are invested in it.

There are many examples of policies, procedures, and protocols that are empty and hollow. Yearly performance evaluations and weekly/monthly supervision meetings are just two examples of a seemingly endless list of missed opportunities in the workplace. As a manager/supervisor, how can you revisit these pieces in order to create large scale credibility? Even if your larger climate/culture isn't jumping in with both feet on this one, is there a way you could increase the relevance around some of these areas, particularly with supervision and performance evaluations/reviews? Being professional means there is value and worth in what is being done in the office, so anything being done has meaning, otherwise you would not do it.

Action: Take Infrastructure Inventory

What are the current policies, procedures, protocols, structures, etc. in place? Of those you identified, can you determine what you have the capacity to shape, impact, or in some way control?

What parts aren't fully being used, or don't have a lot of value but could?

What procedures/protocols/policies would you like to develop?

What would you like your supervisions to be?

What would you like your evaluations to be?

Be specific and concrete. Be sure to use positive language for what you want, not what you don't want it to be!

After exploring the larger context around how the infrastructure can contribute to or support a professional climate and culture, how you can take ownership around building a professional environment?

Here are three tools/strategies to help you become a more Professional leader:

1. Clear on Boundaries

"It was a big mistake to say anything about what I am dealing with around some financial issues, since I make significantly more than the staff. I wish I could take it back."   ~Vice President

"Biggest regret? That's an easy one. I went out with the team and they saw me drink too much. They even have pictures of it. It definitely impacted how they see me. In retrospect, I can't believe I did that and I am embarrassed by my behavior."   ~Director

"Nobody thinks boundaries are a big deal until they are crossed and things seem to fall apart. Leaders need to keep this on the radar all the time, but so many don't and it's unfortunate because you pay dearly for poor boundaries! Trust me!"   ~Executive Director

Poor boundaries can single-handedly undo one's best efforts to be professional. It can cause endless struggles, grief, and regret. It can sabotage the biggest and the best, sending the seemingly infallible in to the abyss of "what not to do." If you want to be revered for your stellar grasp on what it means to be professional, living as the incredible boss you want to be, it is imperative you are clear on the importance of maintaining healthy, consistent boundaries in the workplace.

This is a tough area for people because most people have a powerful desire, whether they will admit it or not, to be liked. Even though they are in charge, leaders still have this urge to connect and be considered part of the team. Although the leader is capable of connecting, and certainly can be in a position to be liked, the nature of the position of a leader precludes the capacity to ever fully assimilate into the group. The role of the leader is to lead the group, so this absence of equality means there will never be reciprocity in this relationship, ensuring there will never be full acceptance into a group. You cannot run the group while simultaneously holding a place in the group, although many have certainly led a valiant effort to prove this theory wrong. Learn from their misery. It cannot be done.

The unequal power balance in the relationship between a leader and the team renders the relationship a clearly defined, non-negotiable, one-way street. It can never be a two-way street because it is within the scope of your job to evaluate, write up, put on probation, or terminate people. You have a say in salary, time off, promotions, and schedules. You have the capacity to impact the trajectory of someone's professional path, which means you have power over them. Leaders who can remember the importance of this power imbalance do very well. They understand the precarious balance of the position, and the need to always respect this dynamic by maintaining clear boundaries.

One the other side of this equation are leaders who disregard or forget this power imbalance. They have ongoing issues, struggles, and challenges with their teams. Refusing to acknowledge the "power over" angle wreaks havoc with teams, but it does a number on the leaders as well! It is important to always remember the people you supervise are not your peers or your equals, so they are not your friends. The workplace is not where you "tell all" about your life. Here is a good benchmark for sharing: If it's something you wouldn't tell a child, or the stranger behind you in line at the grocery store, then please do not tell it to the people you supervise. This means there is never a time to show how well you can hold your alcohol by demonstrating how many shots you can still do, or share the sordid details of your dating life, your horrific divorce, or your escalating financial troubles.

You are there to support, encourage, inspire, and hold accountable. You are not there to make friends or be friends. People will argue against this with attempts to prove they are different, and that they can walk that line with grace and ease, but it gets really hard to write someone up on Monday morning after they watched you stumble around in a drunken stupor Friday night. It doesn't sit well with people when they have heard you complain about your finances for months, knowing you make at least $30,000 more than they do, then you tell them there is a freeze on raises and bonuses for the indefinite future. Your job titles certainly are not blurry; make sure your relationship lines are not either.

Some leaders will say they have things going on in life, and it's only natural to let the team know. There is a difference between letting people know a snippet of what is happening, like you are dealing with health issues with your mother, but it's another to use work as a platform to process your personal life. Many will say that would never happen, or wonder who would actually do that, but unfortunately it happens frequently. Those bad boundaries are doing damage on every level with leaders and teams. When leaders bring issues/drama from their daily lives into the workplace, all it does is erode their credibility and diminish their capacity to lead. Bottom line: You have friends, don't you? If you need to talk, talk to them. If you're going to go out, go out with them, and focus on being a powerful leader for your team.

The model below was developed to help people visualize the difference in the two kinds of boundaries. It's helpful to illustrate the line between the two to solidify the importance of understanding how boundaries shift as relationships shift; all relationships are not created equal.

Understanding Boundaries

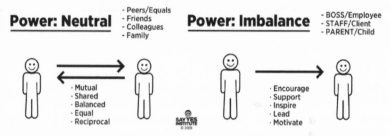

Power: Neutral
- Peers/Equals
- Friends
- Colleagues
- Family

· Mutual
· Shared
· Balanced
· Equal
· Reciprocal

Power: Imbalance
- BOSS/Employee
- STAFF/Client
- PARENT/Child

· Encourage
· Support
· Inspire
· Lead
· Motivate

Action: Set Better Boundaries

Reflect on your boundaries with different people in your world. Think about relationships in your personal life (friends, family, neighbors, acquaintances), then think about your professional relationships. How would you categorize the power you hold in those relationships? What relationships have neutral/equal power, and where is the power balance unequal? Why is it important to be aware of boundaries? What is the impact?

Define: WHAT

What kind of boundaries do you want to have as a leader? What does it look like for you to consistently maintain professional boundaries? What will you do/not do?

> **What is your specific, concrete, and measurable goal? (How much, how many, by when?)**

> **What would having this mean to you, or do for you?**

> **What is of value to you about this goal?**

> **What does your goal look like when you've reached it, or how will you know when you have reached it?**

Clarify: WHY

Why do you want to create and maintain professional boundaries with your team? Why does this matter?

Why are you invested in reaching your goal?

Why do you feel a sense of passion, commitment, or alignment around this goal?

Why is this goal a priority for you?

Why would reaching this goal be of value to you, your work, or your life?

Implement: HOW

How will you develop and maintain professional boundaries with your team? How will take steps and do things differently in order to ensure you are consistently able to fulfill your commitment to this goal?

How will you develop a plan and timeline for reaching this goal?

How will you know you have achieved this goal?

How will you address any barriers, challenges, or obstacles?

How/ to whom will you be accountable?

2. Clear on Ownership

"Every meeting it seems like I am telling them over and over they need to take initiative, take a lead, take ownership and every meeting they look back at me with blank stares. It's getting so old and I don't know how else to say it!"   ~Associate Director

"All I will say is the level of apathy here is toxic. I'm not sure why, but it is. I'm throwing my hands up on this one." ~Unit Manager
"I dread running meetings here. I've never seen a group like this. Nobody seems to say a thing, except for me. I keep presenting ideas but they never go anywhere."   ~Manager

We have established it is important to support professionalism by the infrastructure in place around policies/procedures, etc., and by leaders having clear boundaries. The next level of professionalism expands to focus on how the leader develops the participation, or ownership, of the team. How do you ensure people are actively engaged, individually and collectively, on every level? How do you develop ownership around goals, initiatives, projects, vision, mission, and future growth or expansion?

Leaders seem to consistently struggle with this piece. Many report feeling like no matter how many times they say it's important, or how much they want or need people to take initiative and ownership, nothing happens. Why is it so complicated? Why do so many managers complain about this piece? Are there just a lot of leaders that got a bad hand and were dealt a lazy, disconnected, and apathetic team?

The good news is it's not a flawed team, it's a just flawed approach. Leaders need to revisit the strategy they are using to engage the team and build ownership. They need to remember nobody is ever going own something s/he did not put anything IN to. People need to contribute something to the process in order to ever own the process.

People think you can expect, demand, or mandate ownership. You can certainly expect, demand, or mandate that people complete tasks, perform duties, and maintain perfunctory participation, but if you want authentic, engaged, electric, inspired, and incredible participation that comes with owning something, you need to give people the opportunity to put something in! The Ownership Model helps illustrate the process of how to shift a culture/climate to become more engaged and participatory.

The Ownership Model was created to help leaders understand how important involvement is to creating and supporting ownership. It illustrates how the catalyst for building ownership originates from INput. INput provides people with the opportunity to share their thoughts, feelings, experiences, suggestions, and insights.

Follow the flow of this model and notice now this INput immediately translates to an increased INterest in what is happening, how it is happening, and when it is happening. As that INterest builds, there is a natural and authentic INvestment in the process. That INvestment leads to the desire to have additional INput, which leads to an ever expanding INterest and fully engaged INvestment. What develops as that cycle goes around and around? A genuine, engaged, electric Ownership! When people are engaged and put something IN to the process, it expands and becomes internalized as the elusive state of Ownership so many leaders crave.

You can tell, or yell, or demand ownership, but you aren't going to ever get it. You can want it, need it, and beg for it, but people don't own something they haven't contributed to. Human nature doesn't work that way. This applies to a room full of 7 year olds or a room full of 50-somethings. Participation is foundational to the process, but for whatever reason, people are resistant to building in that participation. It could be fear, or intimidation, or laziness, but the process you use matters. Pay attention to how you engage staff. Support people to put something IN, and notice how incredible it is to experience the magic that comes with individual and collective ownership. As a leader, it doesn't get much better, or cooler, than this!

Action: Assessing Ownership

Describe what the current climate is around ownership with the team. Is there a difference around individual ownership, and collective ownership? Where is it working, and where could it be improved?

Define: WHAT

What do you want to do to support increased ownership? What situations or circumstances (meetings, supervisions, trainings, etc.) could benefit from increased INput from the team?

What is your specfic, concrete, and measurable goal?

What would having this mean to you, or do for you?

What is of value to you about this goal?

What does your goal look like when you've reached it?

Clarify: **WHY**

Why is it important for you to increase the individual and/or collective ownership of the team? Why does this matter to you?

Why are you invested in reaching your goal?

Why do you feel a sense of passion, commitment, or alignment around this goal?

Why is this goal a priority for you?

Why would reaching this goal be of value to you, your work, or your life?

Implement: HOW

How will you take action to consistently build in opportunities for people to have INput? How will you start this initiative, and how will you involve or include other?

How will you develop a plan and timeline for reaching this goal?

How will you know you have achieved this goal?

How will you address any barriers, challenges, or obstacles?

How/ to whom will you be accountable?

3. Clear on Conflict

"There is nothing more stressful to me than conflict. I know people look to me to handle things, but to be honest I really hate it and will do absolutely anything to avoid it."   ~Team Leader

"When there are issues within the team, my first inclination is to deny anything is wrong and hope it disappears!"   ~Coordinator

"Conflict makes me nervous. I'm not sure what to do and I'm scared if I get involved I could make things worse."   ~Associate Director

The final area of focus around being professional is dedicated to what you do when things get hard, or challenging, or don't go as you had hoped, planned, or expected. As a leader, how do you handle conflict? What kind of environment are people working in? Is it one where conflict brews over time, eroding relationships and trust, until things become intolerable and something big happens? Is the environment a breeding ground for denial, avoidance, resentment, anger, and distrust? Is conflict the unspoken plague keeping you awake at night, as it systematically eats away at the foundation of your team, department, or group?

Or is conflict actually viewed as nothing more than a simple difference of opinion, which is acknowledged, embraced, and in some ways celebrated because it reflects engagement, participation, passion, and investment? Can you even imagine how incredible that kind of climate would be, for staff and for leaders? How would that paradigm shift serve to redefine this very scary word and deflate it back down to the essence of what it really is, which is simply a difference of opinions?

Conflict is a scary concept because people have had such upsetting, unhealthy, disturbing, and dysfunctional experiences with what it means, what it represents, what it does, and what it creates. Generally speaking, the people you are in charge of leading and inspiring are not coming to work every day with extensive lifetime experiences and histories full of healthy, thoughtful, reflective, and respectful strategies to handle conflict. Many times in training we will talk about how people do the best they can, based on what they have, which is especially important to remember with conflict. It's not like people are saving their best moves, and most evolved strategies, tools, and approaches to life. They aren't holding back the good stuff with their conflict-resolution skills; you are getting the best they have to give.

This is an important topic in professional arenas because the stress, fear, and anxiety people associate with conflict is going to be just as present in a work situation as it would be if it happened in their personal lives. If you are a leader/supervisor know you will inevitably be in a position to deal with, handle, and address conflict within a team. As you may already know, things can go to a bad place very fast, and this is certainly not an issue that a leader can successfully hide from or ignore. It's important you become adept at handling conflict. It would be even better if you could go beyond "handling it" and develop the remarkable skill to acknowledge, embrace, and celebrate any time there is a difference of opinions with the team!

When people proudly share they have not experienced conflict at work, it's concerning, because a lack of conflict is often an indication that people just don't care or are pretty disinvested. If people are disconnected, or feel they have no position, no value, or no voice, they say very little. As a leader, it is up to you to pay attention to the atmosphere of participation you are creating and maintaining. It is going to be on you to help shift the implications of conflict within your team, but know your efforts will have tremendous benefit.

In your quest to redefine and expand the concept of conflict, it requires you explore what conflict means to you. If you are like most people, this isn't a benign, easy, unencumbered topic. What if you stepped away from your present framework on conflict and you explored a new angle? What if you embraced a whole new paradigm on what conflict represents? What if your new position contained an inherently positive paradigm of what conflict means, and what conflict can do? Try this angle on and see what you think!

A New Understanding on Conflict

Conflict is a powerful testament to a dynamic, talented, and vibrant team. Conflict means:

>> 1. People care enough about the situation to have an opinion.

>> 2. People care enough abou the situation to take a position.

>> 3. People care enough about the situation to be invested in the outcome.

As a leader, all three of those are positives, with the capacity to contribute to the team, the work, and the overall mission/vision of your agency, program, or business. Remember, you are modeling how to redefine conflict and showing people what it looks like when you are not scared of it, you don't run from it, and you don't deny it. You are showing people what can happen when you acknowledge, embrace, and celebrate it!

As a leader, you can be swimming in this new perspective, and you might even be making progress with how the team is interpreting and experiencing conflict, but that won't help you with concrete strategies to work through it when it actually happens on the team. As the leader, how do you successfully support people to move through diverse opinions, insights, perspectives, beliefs, or positions, and reach the shared goal beyond their differences?

Simply celebrating conflict isn't going to resolve it, so what else can you do? You give people the skills and tools to work through it successfully, starting with the Conflict GPS model.

Conflict GPS: Directions to Resolve Conflict

G: **Goal**
Acquire?
Accomplish?
Achieve?

Name the shared goal.

SAY YES INSTITUTE
© 2010

P: **Position**

You   Other

Name the differing opinions, beliefs, or perspectives creating the conflict.

S: **Solution**
? ? ?

Name the possible solutions to resolve conflict and reach shared goal.

This easy-to-use, easy-to-remember model was created to provide teams with a common language and shared tool to move through their differences of opinion. It is important for people to shape conflict resolution by first naming their shared goal. Conflict often serves as a catalyst to instantly position people in an automatic adversarial or competitive position. This happens because people forget, or overlook, the fact that they actually have a shared goal. It's often helpful for groups to start with, "same shirts, same team," to help people remember they are actually on the same side, with a shared goal. They are not enemies, competitors, or rivals. The first step typically helps shift and reframe the energy, deflating the high emotions that quickly surface whenever a real or perceived conflict emerges.

It is worth mentioning sometimes there is an interesting variable uncovered at the first step; the people who are in conflict actually do not have a shared goal. This lack of an overlap means, from the outset, they are not in the same conversation, which means there is no chance for resolving it. The first step is not a tedious waste of time, as it will illuminate any fundamental "miss" in communication or understanding. If that "miss" is not addressed, the parties will be in for a long and futile exchange, with no chance for resolution, because at the core, they do not hold a shared goal.

The next step, after ensuring and establishing a shared goal, is to have people name their positions. This isn't about proving you are right and the other person is wrong, it is to illustrate there are many different paths to reaching resolution. For many people, conflict brings up very strong feelings, interrupting one's ability to acknowledge other possibilities, positions, or perspectives. Taking time and making space to name the differing positions is a powerful way to review possible options. Again, it is a helpful reminder for people to keep revisiting the philosophy of, "same shirts, same team." There are always different options and opinions on how to achieve a goal, but when both people remember they have a vested interest in reaching the goal it helps keep emotions in check. When people remain calm, engaged, and invested, they stay connected to the process as they explore different perspectives and possibilities.

The final step is focused on identifying possible solutions to resolve or rectify the differences. If there is an agreed-upon shared goal, and an understanding of the different positions, there will be a greater likelihood of openness to exploring solutions. When people are at the point of looking at different solutions they are often ready to compromise as they identify the action needed to reach the shared goal. Typically, by the end of the conversation, people are feeling connected to the shared goal, heard by the other person, and in a positive position to reach some level of resolution around their difference of opinions.

Currently, the concept of conflict may have a negative connotation with your team; as a leader, you play a pivotal role in helping them to expand their understanding of what conflict can mean. As a leader, you are modeling and teaching how the team could effectively and successfully navigate differences of opinion. Being professional comes with a lot of expectations for how you will gracefully handle workplace situations, however, as you know, there is definitely extra attention paid to how you handle challenges. For most leaders, conflict is typically the biggest challenge they face at work.

As a leader, you are committed to fostering an actively engaged team, with all members sharing ideas, suggestions, insights, experiences, and opinions. Because of your commitment to active participation, you are invested in maintaining a professional work environment that consistently embraces and supports effective, healthy, and successful conflict resolution.

Action: Assessing Conflict

Currently, how to you handle and/or respond to conflict? Take an inventory of what it means to you, and how your experiences and beliefs about conflict with conflict impacts the team. What do you do when it happens? How do you handle it? What do you say?

Conflict: Insights, Thoughts, Reflections

Define: WHAT

What would it look like if you redefined conflict and held a more positive perception of what it means to have a difference of opinions in the workplace?

What is your specific, concrete, and measurable goal? (How much, how many, by when?)

What would having this mean to you, or do for you?

What is of value to you about this goal?

What does your goal look like when you've reached it, or how will you know when you have reached it?

Clarify: **WHY**

Why are you committed to expanding your comfort with conflict? Why does this matter? Why will this be beneficial to your team?

Why are you invested in reaching your goal?

Why do you feel a sense of passion, commitment, or alignment around this goal?

Why is this goal a priority for you?

Why would reaching this goal be of value to you, your work, or your life?

Implement: HOW

How will you be a leader around reframing conflict? How will you take action on this initiative, as you shift the current perception of what conflict is, and what it means?

How will you develop a plan and timeline for reaching this goal?

How will you know you have achieved this goal?

How will you address any barriers, challenges, or obstacles?

How/ to whom will you be accountable?

9 YOU'RE NEW AT THIS ...

> *"The person who knows HOW will always have a job.*
> *The person who knows WHY will always be his boss."*
> ~Alanis Morissette

Special Focus: New Supervisors, Managers, and Leaders

This final chapter gives an extra highlight to supervisors/managers/leaders just "out of the gates" and new to being accountable for other people. It's important to note being "new" to the field of supervising does not necessarily correlate to one's chronological age. Some are new to supervising at 25 years old, while others are new to it at 53 years old. This section is for those beginning the journey and interested in a few more tips, thoughts, and suggestions on how to be successful in this new phase of leadership.

Out of the Gates: *Powerful*

>> Trust you have the capacity to lead. This is one of the biggest pieces new supervisors struggle with and in the absence of this trust, they are hesitant, uncertain, or overwhelmed, making it hard to move through the days feeling powerful.

>> Understand confidence does not automatically accompany your new job title, so dig deep and find it. On days you don't feel it, dig deeper. It's on you to find it and feel it.

>> Unless your family owns the company, chances are you got this position because the hiring team believed you were the best person for the job and have the education, experience, and capacity to succeed. Believe them-- then prove them right.

>> Get clear on what you are bringing to this position. The world doesn't keep a running list of all of your impressive qualifications, or everything fabulous about you, so you'd better keep it. You are great at a lot of things,

and you have a lot to offer. Your capacity to be viewed as powerful and capable of leading a team hinges on your ability to believe it.

>> People aren't going to adore you, follow you, or respect you, for your title. People adore, follow, and respect people who are solid, clear, consistent, and focused.

>> You do not know all you need to know, and this will not be an effortless transition, but you can do it. There will be ongoing gaps in what you know, and although you may encounter a significant learning curve, remember it is possible to simultaneously hold what you know, with what you have yet to learn. You may not have all the details of the job, the team, or the work that is being done, but you do have the education, experience, capacity, foundation, skills, etc., to support this team to greatness. You will make mistakes, you will miss the mark, you will have gaps in what you know, and that's ok. You may not have it all figured out yet, but know in time you will.

>> Being "new" will be what they see initially, but people quickly move beyond that if you are moving forward. If you're stuck on being "new," then the team will be stuck, too.

>> You know being powerful isn't about power over someone else. Because you are new, you will diligently and tirelessly work to build powerful, positive, and professional relationships with the team, as you model investment, respect, and hard work.

>> You authentically show up, consistently offering the best you have. You become more powerful as you grow and learn, owning your skills/ strengths while supporting others to do the same.

Being powerful takes a little getting used to, but you've got this one.

Is there anything else you want to remember and/or add about being *Powerful*?

Out of the Gates: *Positive*

You understand people don't always love their jobs, or the business/agency they work for, and they aren't all going to adore their bosses or the leadership in charge. As the leader, what are you going to do with that? Are you joining them? You will need to decide how you are going to move through your days if/when the office culture leans to the negative side. You don't need to lead daily workshops on being positive, or conduct hourly cheers in the office around motivation and morale, but you do need to decide, on a daily basis, how you are going to handle your approach to work and the people on your team.

>> You are dialed in to the fact that not all offices are filled with positive people, in a positive culture, focused on looking for what is right, what is working, what is getting done, what is going well, and you get that there are a lot of negative environments, unhealthy dynamics, and toxic people out there. What does this mean for a new supervisor? A lot. There are countless examples of "good" people going "bad" in "bad" environments. If people aren't paying attention, this shift can happen quickly, quietly, and under the radar. Be clear on where you stand, intentional in your focus/energy, and regularly check in to make sure your outlook/perspective is where you want it to be.

>> You understand you can be positive, even when others aren't, or can't, or won't. You are new at this but you model how to be excited, optimistic, invested in the possibility/potential of what can be and not hyper-focused on what's flawed, broken, or missing.

>> Your positive energy can inspire and motivate others, and you use that power on a daily basis to benefit the team and the work you are doing together.

>> You realize it's not your job to make other people be positive; you can only control how you move through this world. There are people out there 34 years, 56 years, or 68 years deep in to living life finding everything wrong, everywhere they go, and they're certainly not going to change because of you. The key, especially for a leader, is to not let someone else's negative journey hijack your positive approach to work or life!

>> Even though you may not have tons of experience, you already know being negative erodes your credibility, your power, your impact, your success, and does a number on your capacity to enjoy life.

>> You understand how you move through the world has far-reaching ripple effects, so when you choose where your focus will be, you choose wisely. You know this position is giving you the opportunity to lay an amazing foundation on which to build your reputation, and your career, and you're going to take full advantage of it.

Being positive inspires people, making you a people magnet, which is magical when you're the leader.

Is there anything else you want to remember and/or add about being *Positive*?

Out of the Gates: *Professional*

Being an example, or a model, for the right way to do things isn't always easy or effortless, but it matters and it's worth it, so you will put in the daily effort to do it.

>> You understand every day isn't going to be amazing, and every interaction, meeting, supervision, evaluation, etc., isn't going to embody perfection. Sometimes you will make hard decisions, and many times you will be challenged. People aren't always going to like you, approve of your decisions, or support your actions. Remember to trust yourself when things aren't easy, because difficulties don't necessarily mean you are doing it wrong. Being professional means you are doing the hard stuff with grace, clarity, integrity, consistency, and a sense of fairness.

>> Maya Angelou said, "I've learned that people will forget what you said, people will forget what you did, but people will never forget how you made them feel." As a leader, it is on you to ensure your team feels respected, valued, appreciated, and supported. This doesn't mean you have a permissive, dismissive, or lax environment that lends itself to chaos or an overall lack of productivity. It means your investment in the positive, and commitment to recognizing the value and contribution of each member of the team, translates to a phenomenal platform of loyalty, investment, and high-caliber work!

>> You have friends, and they are all people you cannot and do not have the capacity to write up, reprimand, promote, or pay. You actually have a lot of friends, and every day you head into work remembering that although you may really like the people greeting you, they are not your friends. You consistently maintain healthy and professional boundaries with the team. Partying, drinking, relationships, over-sharing and disclosures around trauma/drama in your personal life are categorized in your "what not to do as a supervisor" list! Your personal life may not always be neat or orderly and that's ok. Life isn't an endless array of Kodak moments. Sometimes life can be a big mess, with a lot that can and will go wrong. Just make sure the people helping you clean up the "mess" are your equals: your friends, your family, or your peers. The biggest landmine for new supervisors tends to be struggles with boundaries. Never let your professional image, reputation, or credibility be diminished, damaged, or destroyed by struggles in your personal life. Once people know, they will always know and remember. And, most importantly, what people remember, they share. One time, one night, one bad decision has done a number

on many supervisors. Learn from them and keep your boundaries clear, tight, and consistent.

>> You are the supervisor today, but what would happen if, in the future, you found yourself in a different role or position with someone you used to supervise? Imagine you, or someone in your life, interviewing for a job and the person making the final decision was someone from your team today. Would that be a horrific nightmare, or an unexpected delight? It happens, perhaps more than you would think. When you are professional, it means you will be able to cross paths, directly or indirectly, in any context, at any point in the future, and it would be a pleasant surprise. Being professional ensures a level of respect and appreciation capable of transcending your current roles/positions and qualifies you as a leader people will always remember fondly. A powerful, positive, professional leader, also known as *The Dream Boss*.

Being professional isn't a quality that comes with a title; it happens whenever someone is looked to as an example for how to do it right. You're new at this, but you will be that example.

Is there anything else you want to remember and/or add about being *Professional*?

10 CLOSING

"The game of life is the game of boomerangs.
Our thoughts, deeds, and words return to us sooner or later,
with astounding accuracy."
~Florence Shinn

To summarize, here's what we know: As a manager, leader, supervisor, boss, director, whatever your title may be, you want to be successful. You know your role is to inspire, motivate, support, encourage, and lead the group in a powerful, positive, and professional way. You want to do the best job possible, for you and for the team, because your work is a significant part of your time, your efforts, and your journey in life. You deserve to have the skills and tools to learn from, grow from, and ultimately enjoy, the people you are leading, managing, and working with.

By nature of your role, on a daily basis you have a tremendous impact on people. You are in the remarkable position of being able to teach, support, and inspire the people around you, effectively modeling how to be a successful leader. Give yourself credit for exploring how to build new skills and try different approaches in your work with people, because not everyone is willing to take on that kind of growth. Congratulations for your commitment, and your effort. It will make a difference to you, as well as all of those fortunate enough to cross paths with you!

In closing, here are a few final tips for you to remember, reflecting thoughts from this book, as well as additional snippets gathered from years of supporting people to build emotional intelligence skills.

The Dream Boss knows...

>> You can't give what you don't have. If you feel like you're running on empty, you are. Refill, refuel, replenish. Take care of yourself, for you and for all the people in your world.

>> You won't know if something works, or doesn't work, until you try it. Over the years, countless people have heard me remind them, "Clarity doesn't come from sitting on the couch!" At some point, it's time to stop analyzing, stop assessing, stop thinking, and start doing.

>> You will get more mileage out of taking a minute to think, "What is my goal in this situation?" than you will by any book, workshop, coaching, or training. In any situation, spending a few seconds to get clear on your goal helps shift and shape your energy, focus, and plan for action. Being clear on your goal taps into your intrinsic strengths to adeptly handle any situation, even the hard ones.

>> People respond to your energy; make sure you are putting out what you want to get back.

>> Saying "thank you" benefits everyone, but in reality, it does more for you than for the person to whom you're saying it. Every day, as you move through the world, look for ways to say it, a lot.

>> Progress isn't a neat, straight, linear process. It doesn't always follow your plan, and sometimes doesn't even acknowledge you had a plan. Many times, you won't know you've made it until you look back and see it.

>> "Sleeping on it" certainly can help settle your thoughts, but some people seem to be living on bed rest. Contemplation, analysis, and speculation have a lot of people living life on pause.

>> Fear isn't a deal breaker. Remind yourself fear is a positive feeling, because if you are scared, it means you're about to do something new. It will work, and that's great, or it won't, and you'll get feedback about what to do differently next time. Either way, you win.

>> If you are scared and want to move through it, name the worst-case scenario and see if you could live through it. If you could, then you do it. If you couldn't, then perhaps that's a risk you aren't in a position to take right now. It's a miraculous cure for unfounded, limiting, or irrational/illogical fears! You should know, nobody has ever said they could not or would not live through the results of a risk s/he was contemplating.

>> Focusing on the positive will always take you to a better place, and the transport is almost instantaneous.

>> Being positive means people will like you and want to be around you; at home, at work, and in the world, people gravitate to the positive, which includes positive people.

FYI: "People like to be around positive people" may not be universally applicable to exceptionally miserable, negative, or toxic people. Being positive can be somewhat of a repellant for them and they seem to stay away, which isn't necessarily a bad thing.

>> The quality of your life is all about your relationships, at home, at work, and in the world. Be the kind of person people want to be around.

>> For you, and the people you work with, work is one part of life. It's a significant part, but it is not the only part. A balanced life is "macro," meaning you see and hold all parts and find the peace that comes from the perspective of the bigger picture. An unbalanced life is "micro," focused on whatever is wrong, and typically manifests as stress, despair, and anxiety. Remember, if you feel overwhelmed, stressed, or like you're stuck in a negative place, somehow you have lost perspective and have gone "micro." Pick your head up and expand what you are seeing. This doesn't take away what's wrong, but refocusing on the bigger picture of your life reminds you there is still a lot right.

>> Just because you've done it one way for as long as you can remember, it doesn't mean there isn't another way. You are always growing, evolving, learning, and expanding. Life continuously presents opportunities to try on different strategies/approaches/tools to help in your journey, so take advantage of that and use them!

>> Taking five minutes to just sit and take a breath, alone, could make all the difference in your day. This is especially crucial on those days you feel like you absolutely do not have the five minutes to spare.

>> Find the humor in life. There is a lot of funny out there, if you choose to see it. Laughing could quite possibly be the foundation of it all—and what makes life so incredible! So, at home, at work, and in your world, find the humor and laugh.

>> Finally, enjoy your journey to becoming and being … *The Dream Boss*!

Made in the USA
San Bernardino, CA
16 October 2013